HOW TO FIND YOUR BIRTH PARENTS

A GUIDE AND JOURNAL

EMMALINE MACBEATH M.Ed MSM

TRIOMPHE PRESS

ISBN 978-1-958123-12-6
eISBN 978-1-958123-13-3

Printed in the United States of America

This guide is for everyone who is searching for answers

CONTENTS

INTRODUCTION

This guide is for everyone who needs a place to start

Now that you have chosen to begin the journey to discover your family story, you may be asking yourself: "What do I do first?" This guide and journey journal will take you through the steps to finding your birth family. No two stories or journeys are the same. How you choose to complete your search will be a personal choice, but following all of the basic steps in this guide will lead you to the most positive and reliable outcome.

Important Notes

This guide is not meant to replace professional help. You may be one of the lucky ones who is able to complete your search quickly and without help. If not, I urge you to consider hiring a professional genetic genealogist or post-adoption search/DNA specialist who can be an advocate and assistant you on your journey.

I do not recommend starting your birth parent search before you turn the age of eighteen. Privacy laws in most locations will be a hindrance due to your age. Paperwork (including original birth certificates and adoption files) is not available to anyone below the age of eighteen, and in some locations, below the age of twenty-one. The terms of service at the major DNA companies require you to be eighteen years old to submit a DNA sample.

ABOUT THIS GUIDE

Who is This Guide For?

Anyone who is looking for or hoping to confirm one or both birth parents.

Terminology

Any time the word parent, mother, or father is used, this refers to the family you grew up with. Biological family will be referred to as birth parent, birth mother, birth father, or birth family.

How This Guide is Organized

A journey doesn't happen all in one day and if you want to get there faster, it's best taken in the right order instead of wandering from place to place. This guide is divided into three main parts. Each section will guide you from one important step in your journey to the next.

The first section—**First Steps**—will guide you through preparing for your search journey. Don't skip this step or you may find yourself backtracking to complete vital tasks later.

The second section—**Next Steps**—will take you through the core of your journey. This is where you will roll up your sleeves and dig in to the work.

The third section—**Final Steps**—gives you time to process your thoughts and feelings once your birth parents are identified. It will guide you through making new connections if this is your choice.

Throughout the guide, you will be given space to journal your thoughts and feelings.

If you need more space to write, at the back of the guide, you will find additional journal pages. Again, don't skip this step. Searching for birth parents is an emotional journey. Processing your feelings as you go will help you reduce stress and help you know when it may be time for outside help.

At the back of the guide, you will also find a section called "Clues" where you can write down information as you discover it. This will will allow you to gather everything in one place for later when you will need it.

"Expect the best,
plan for the worst,
and prepare to be surprised."
—Author Denis Waitley

FIRST STEPS

The first steps to your search journey are:

1) Set your goals and ask the hard questions
2) Consider professional help
3) Gather clues
4) Take a DNA test

Each of these steps is crucial to the success of your journey. Please don't skip any.

SETTING GOALS

Setting The Goals For Your Journey

The very first, and most important item on your journey to-do list is setting goals. Goals will help guide your actions along the way. If something goes off in a direction you didn't expect, you will have already thought about how to react to it.

Key questions:
- What do I hope will happen at the end of this journey?
- What will I do if things don't turn out as expected?
- To what lengths am I willing to go to get answers?
- How do I feel right now about this journey?
- How open am I willing to be versus how private do I wish to keep my search? (Is this a private journey?)
- Who am I willing to enlist to help me on my journey?

JOURNAL QUESTION 1

What do I hope will happen at the end of this journey?

The number one question you must answer before you begin your journey is: what is your purpose for your search? In other words, what one main expectation do you have? Do you just want names so you can build a family tree and know who your ancestors are? Do you want medical information? Are you hoping to meet some birth family? Do you plan to reach out to your birth family or do you have no wish to do so? Are you looking for closure to your past?

There is absolutely no right or wrong answer to these questions. Your journey is a personal one. It won't look like any other person's journey. Knowing ahead of time what you hope to accomplish will help you to set personal boundaries for your search. For instance, if you already know you don't wish to meet your newly found family, but they ask you to do so, you won't have to think about your answer. You already have it.

Action: Answer question number 1 in your Journey Journal. Add as much specific detail as you can at this time. It's okay if your answers change later as new information comes to light.

Here are some additional questions to help guide you toward answers:

- Do I want family names so I can build a family tree and know who my ancestors are?

- Do I want medical information?

- Am I hoping to meet some biological family?
- Do I want a relationship with my newly found family?
- Do I want closure to my birth story?
- Will I contact my birth parent(s) if they are still living?
- Will I contact other biological family members?

What do I hope will happen at the end of this journey?

_____

_____

_____

_____

_____

_____

_____

_____

_____

_____

_____

_____

_____

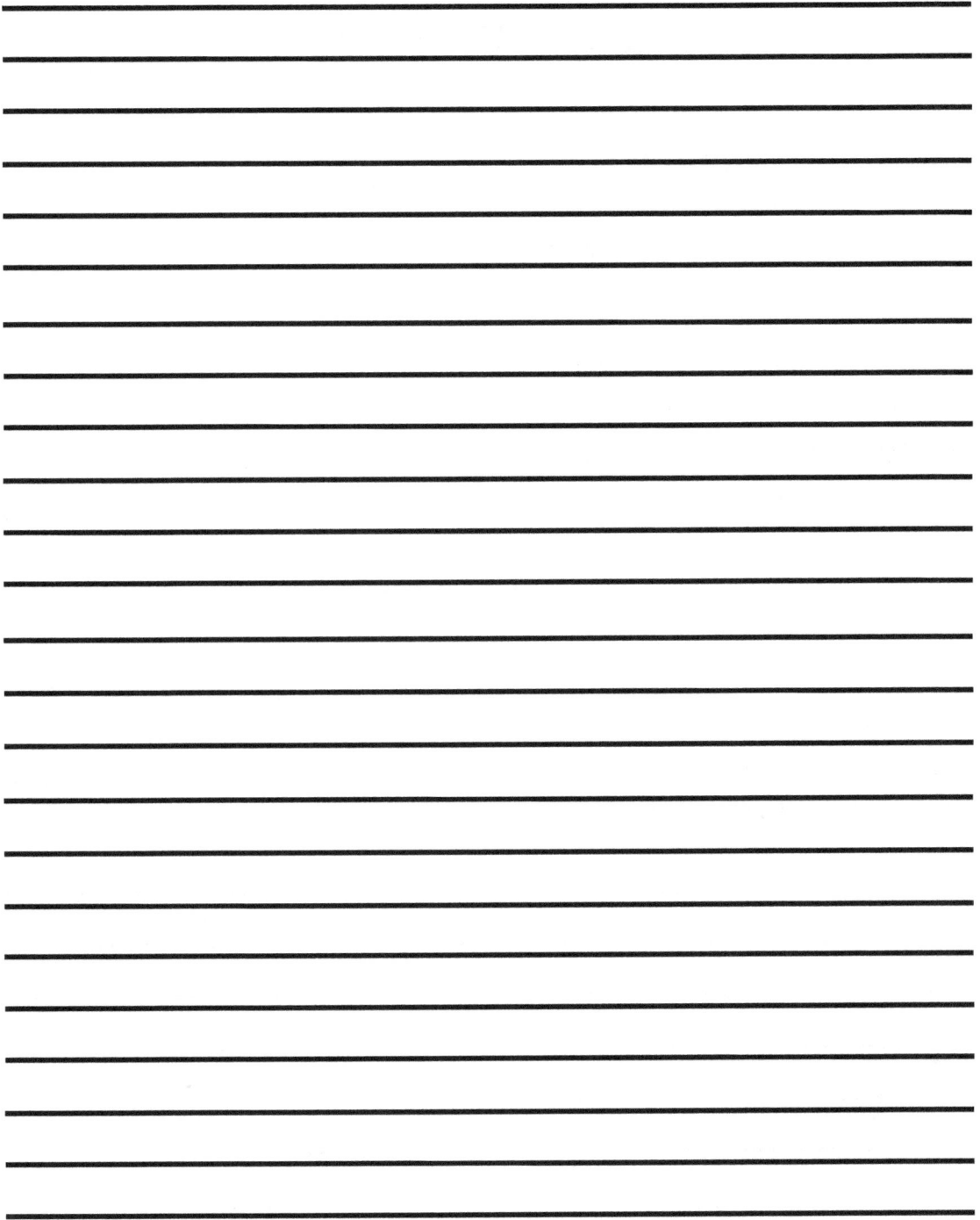

JOURNAL QUESTION 2

How do I feel about this journey?

How are you feeling right now? Are you excited? Nervous? Scared? A little bit of all of the above?

This is a good time to stop and talk about the fact that searching for birth family is first and foremost an emotional journey. Sometimes it feels like an emotional roller coaster. One day you may find out new information that makes you sit up and cheer. Other days you may find out new information that makes you sad or upset.

It's important to stop at every step along the way to ask yourself how you are feeling. Honor those feelings. Give yourself time to work through them before moving forward. It's okay to step away from the search for a time in order to do so.

Action: Answer question number 2 in your Journey Journal. Then continue to ask yourself this question along the way: ***How am I feeling today about the idea of finding my birth family?***

_____

_____

_____

_____

_____

_____

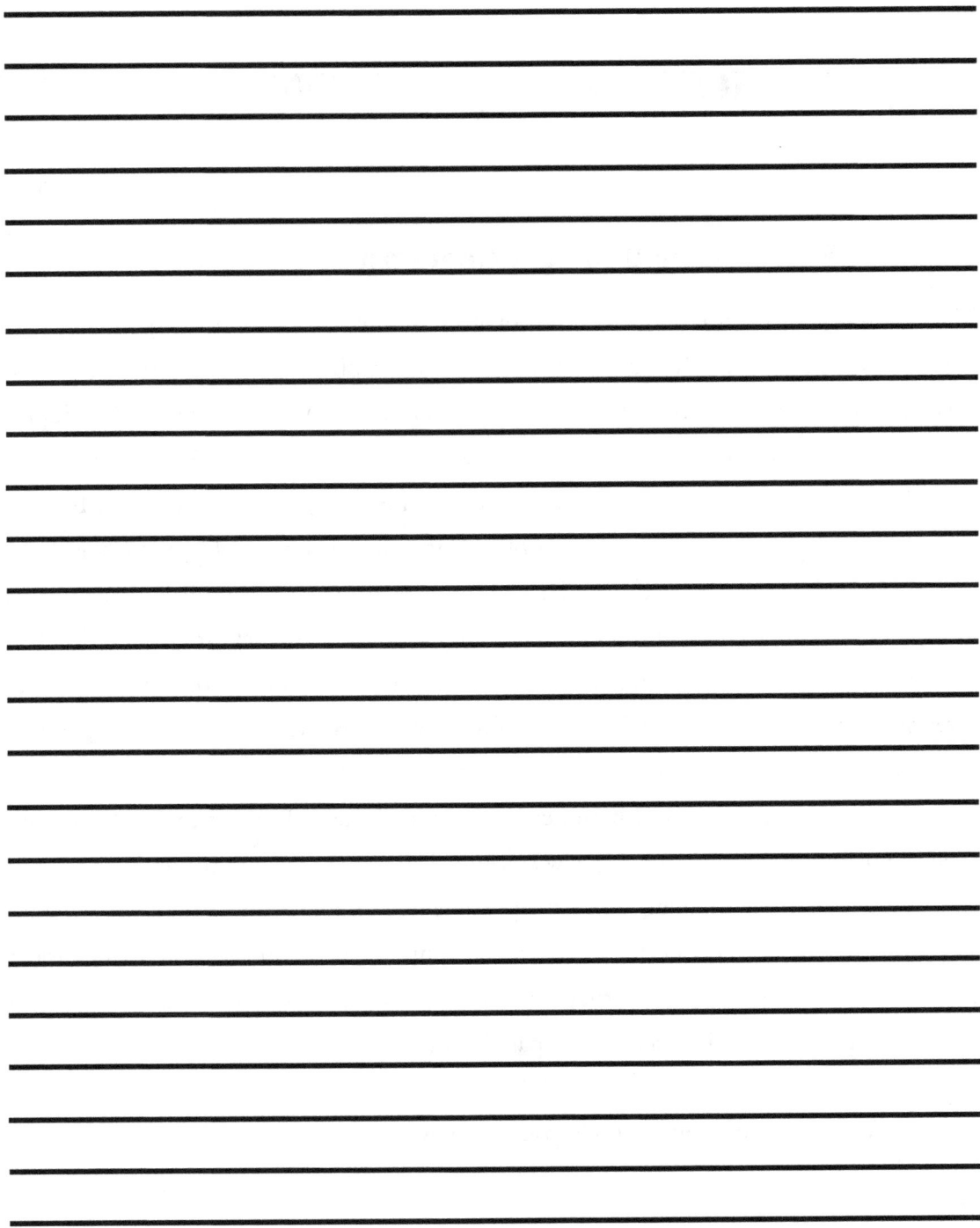

JOURNAL QUESTION 3

What will I do if things do not turn out as expected?

Many searches for birth family end with joyous reunions. The adoptee may find a living parent or two, some half siblings, cousins, nieces and nephews, and aunts and uncles. In this scenario, everyone is thrilled to find each other again. The family welcomes the adoptee with open arms. Hallelujah! We all cheer when we hear these happy stories.

Unfortunately, not every story end this way. Some adoptees find out one or both of their biological parents were not nice people. Or they had serious problems such as drugs and alcohol addictions. Sometimes, the adoptees reach out and the birth family wants absolutely nothing to do with them—afraid they will upset the delicate balance of their family. In some cases, the adoptee was a well kept family secret and the birth family has no intention of opening that locked door for everyone to see. Sometimes a person's conception story was traumatic.

For those not adopted and have newly discovered one or both of their parents isn't their biological parent, there may be new emotional challenges to work through.

Spend some time thinking about the possible outcomes of your search. This doesn't mean you should dwell on all the negatives that could happen, but rather at least consider them at the beginning of your journey. This way, if something negative does come to light or does happen, you will have already prepared yourself.

Action: Answer question number 3 in your Journey Journal.

Here are some additional questions to help guide you to your answers:

- What if I find out something about my family I really didn't want to know?
- What if my birth family wants to welcome me with open arms? Am I comfortable with this level of relationship?
- What will I do if my birth parent(s) end up being people I don't want to know?
- What will I do if my birth family wants nothing to do with me? How will I feel?
- What if I find out there was trauma associated with my conception?
- What if one of my birth parents denies any possibility they could be my parent?
- What if my birth family attempts to take legal action to stop me from finding answers or making contact?
- How will I react if a member of my birth family says mean things to me?
- What if I find out my birth parent(s) has passed away?

_____

_____

_____

_____

_____

_____

_____

_____

_____

_____

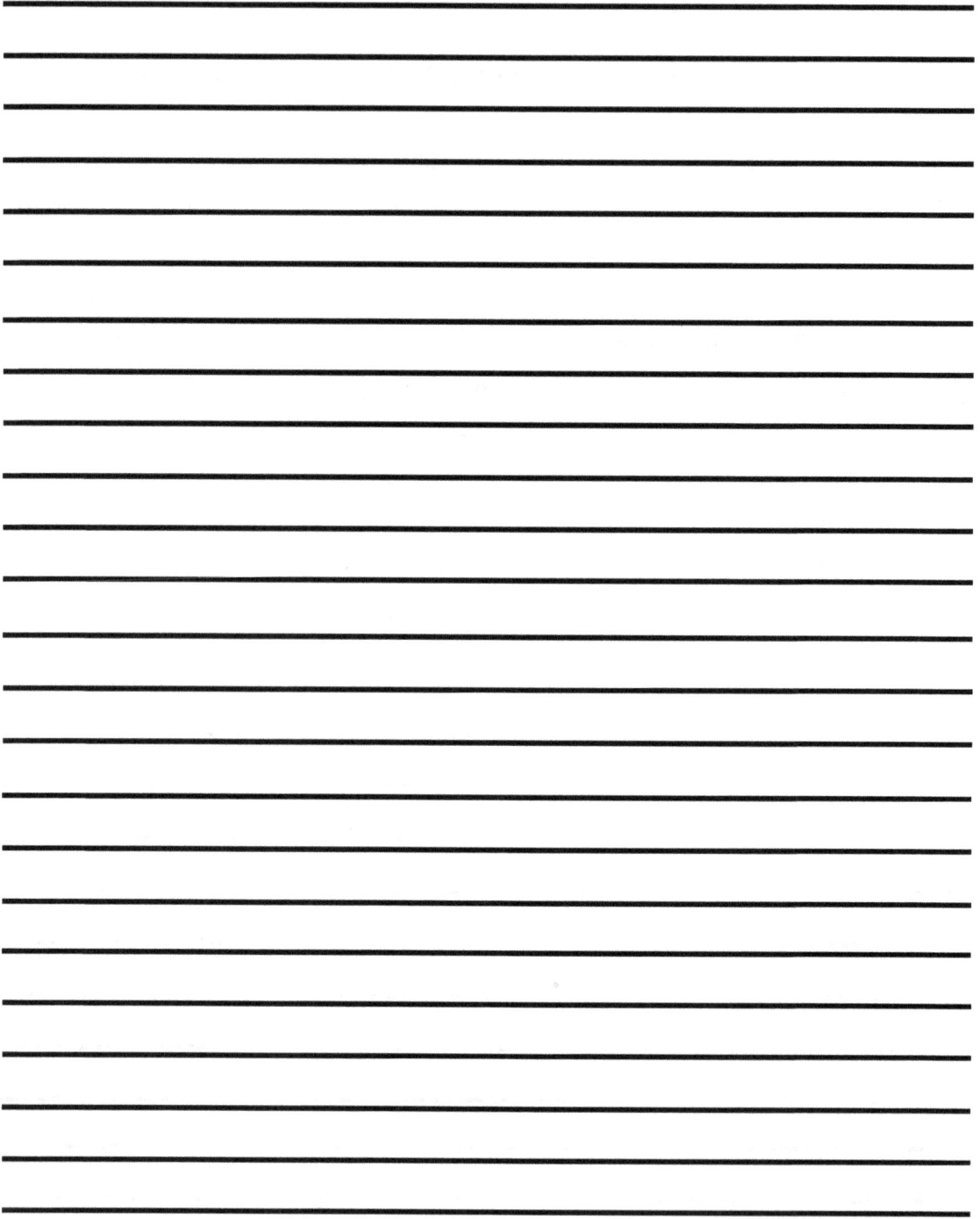

JOURNAL QUESTION 4

Will I tell my family I'm searching?

Some people don't wish to tell their family they are starting a birth parent search for fear the search will hurt them in some way. Keep in mind a couple of things.

- This is your personal search. You have a need to know the answers or you wouldn't have considered this journey in the first place.
- Your family can be your allies in your search.
- If you've done everything you can to reassure your family that your wish to search doesn't mean you love them less, and they are still upset, this is something they have to work through for themselves. You are not responsible for how they feel about the search.

Advice: When talking to your family about your search, tell them your goals, so they will better understand your motivation for beginning this journey.

Action: Answer question number 4 in your Journey Journal.

Here are some additional questions to help guide you to your answers:

- Which family members will I tell?
- How will I tell my family I'm searching?
- What will I do if my mom/dad (or other family member) gets upset about the search?

Follow Up Journal Question 4A: I told my family about my search. How did it go? How did they react? What were the concerns?

_____

_____

_____

_____

_____

_____

_____

_____

_____

_____

_____

_____

_____

_____

_____

_____

_____

_____

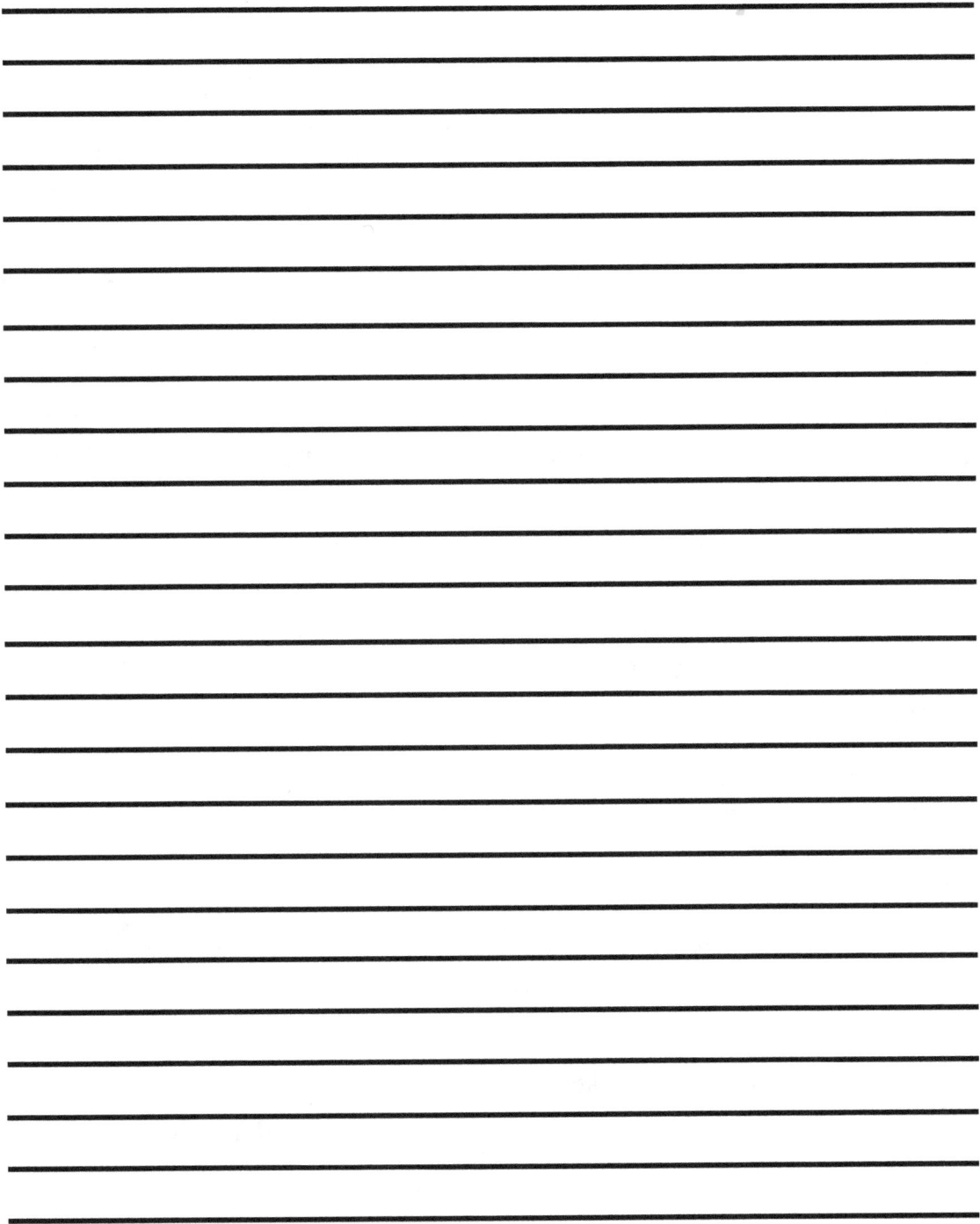

JOURNAL QUESTION 5

To what lengths am I willing to go to get answers?

This sounds like a dramatic question doesn't it? But the bottom line is, how bold are you willing to be? How much money are you willing to spend? How much time will you devote to your search?

Some people are pretty nervous about starting their search and start by dipping their toe into the water so to speak, then step away for a while, and then come back. Rinse and repeat.

Others are all in. They learn all they can, take all the DNA tests, join all the groups, talk to as many people as they can—whatever it takes to find answers right now. Once they find their birth family, they make contact right away.

And then there are those somewhere in the middle.

Which group are you?

Action: Take some time to honestly answer question number 5 about yourself in your Journey Journal.

Here are some additional questions to help guide you to your answers:

- How quickly do I want the answers to my search?
- How much money am I willing to spend on this search?
- How much of my time am I willing to spend on this search?
- Who am I willing to talk to?

- Where am I willing to travel?
- Am I willing to hire someone to help me? If so, do I want to do that now or see how well I do on my own first?
- Am I willing to tell my story to whoever will listen to get answers more quickly?
- Am I willing to make contact with every DNA match I can and every potential family member to get answers?

_____

_____

_____

_____

_____

_____

_____

_____

_____

_____

_____

_____

_____

_____

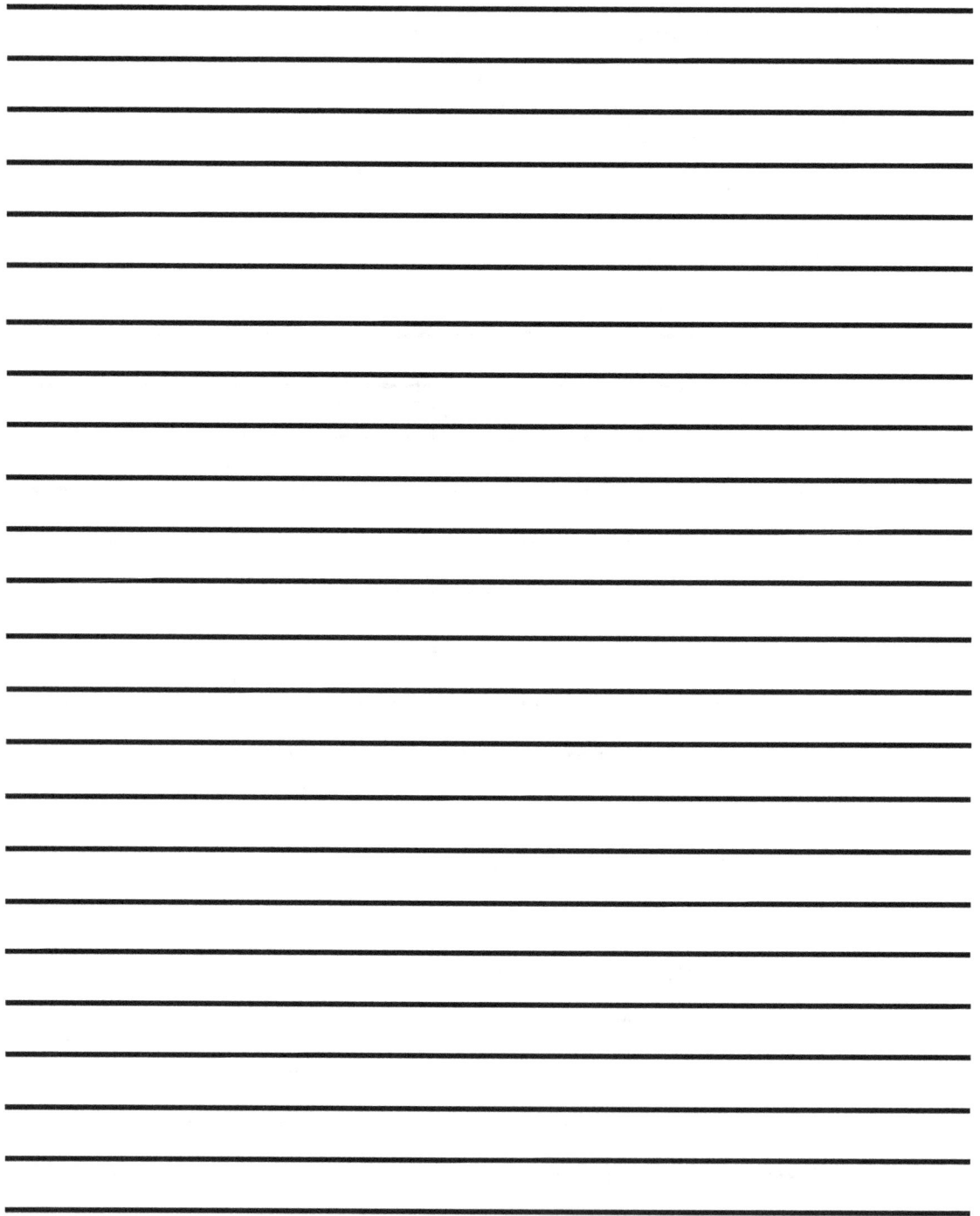

JOURNAL QUESTION 6

How Private do I wish my journey to be?

There are many privacy concerns to take into account when searching for birth family. You need to consider them ahead of time so you are prepared for how much you are willing to share with strangers who may (or may not) be able to help you on your journey.

Many adoptees are willing to share their birth date and birth location, along with the hospital they were born in and any information they might know about their birth family. I often see people paste this information all across social media and a variety of websites. The problem with this is identify theft is a real concern. Scammers scrape websites for this kind of information on a regular basis and use it to hurt people. I'm going to boldly recommend you don't do this, even in a private group. Once that information is posted on the internet, it can't be taken back.

However, what you tell a stranger privately on a case by case basis is up to you.

I've worked with people who will share only the most basic of information, don't want to reach out to DNA matches or other potential family members, and even in some cases, won't share their real name.

Then I've worked with people who will share everything they know about themselves and will talk to anyone who will listen.

And of course most fall somewhere in between.

In order to get help on your journey, you *will* need to share some information with some people.

Action: Answer question number 6 in your Journey Journal.

Here are some additional questions to help guide you to your answers:

- If adopted, will I tell DNA matches I'm adopted when sending a message for more information?
- If not adopted, will I tell DNA matches why I'm looking for more information about my family?
- How much information will I share about myself to my DNA matches?
- Will I tell my story to strangers in groups (such as Facebook) if they are willing to help me?
- How much about myself am I willing to share with newly found family?

_____

_____

_____

_____

_____

_____

_____

_____

_____

_____

_____

_____

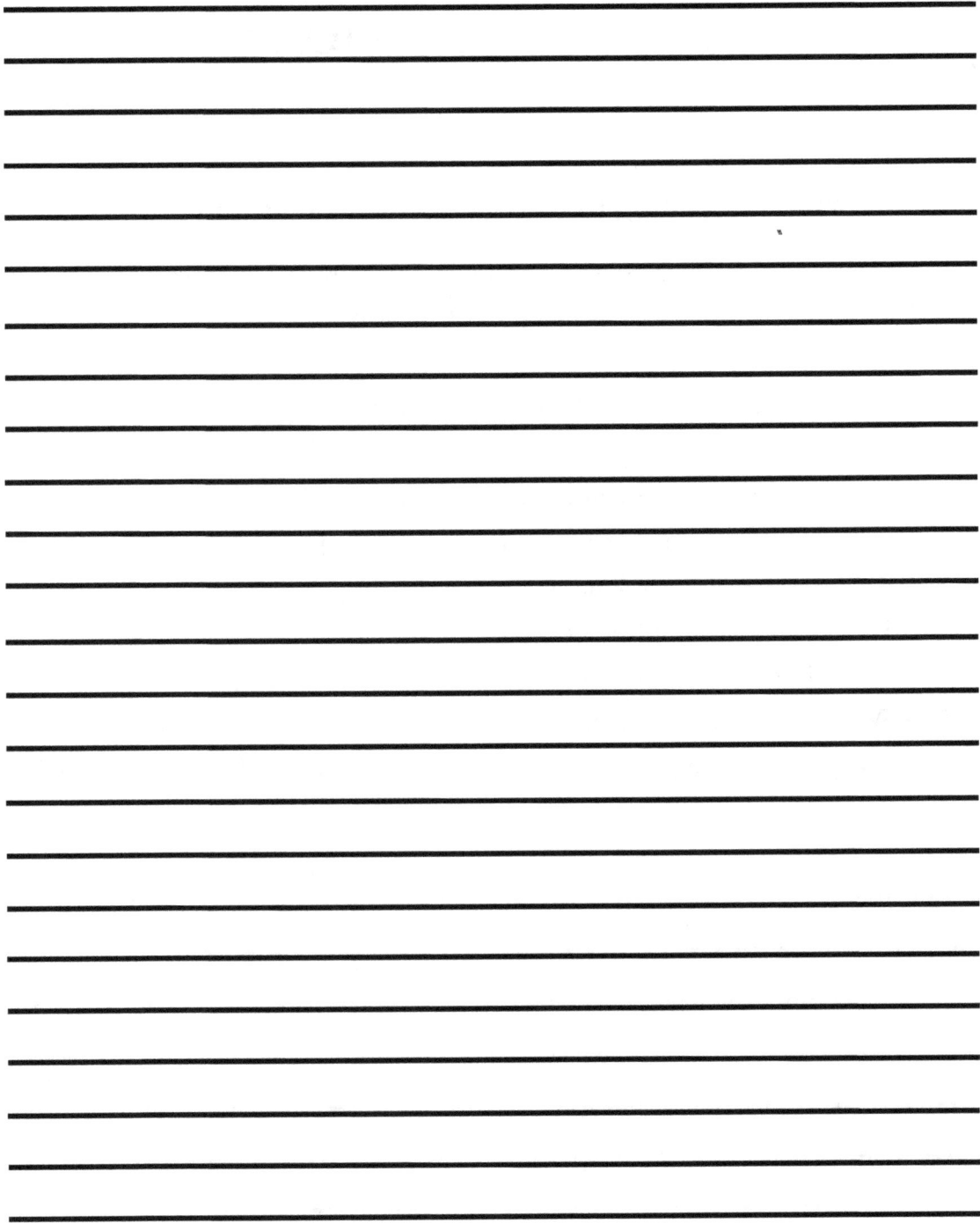

JOURNAL QUESTION 7

Who am I willing to enlist to help me on my journey?

There are many different aspects to a search for birth family. And let's face it, getting help might ease the way. But who are you willing to ask for help?

Action: Answer question number 7 in your Journey Journal.

Here are some additional questions to help guide you to your answers:

- Do I want to pay for professional help or see how far I can get on my own first?
- Am I willing to trust a volunteer search angel to help?
- Do I want my family members to help?
- Would I let a complete stranger help?
- What if that stranger is a DNA match?
- What if that stranger is a kind person who wants to help, but has no DNA connection to me?

_____

_____

_____

_____

_____

_____

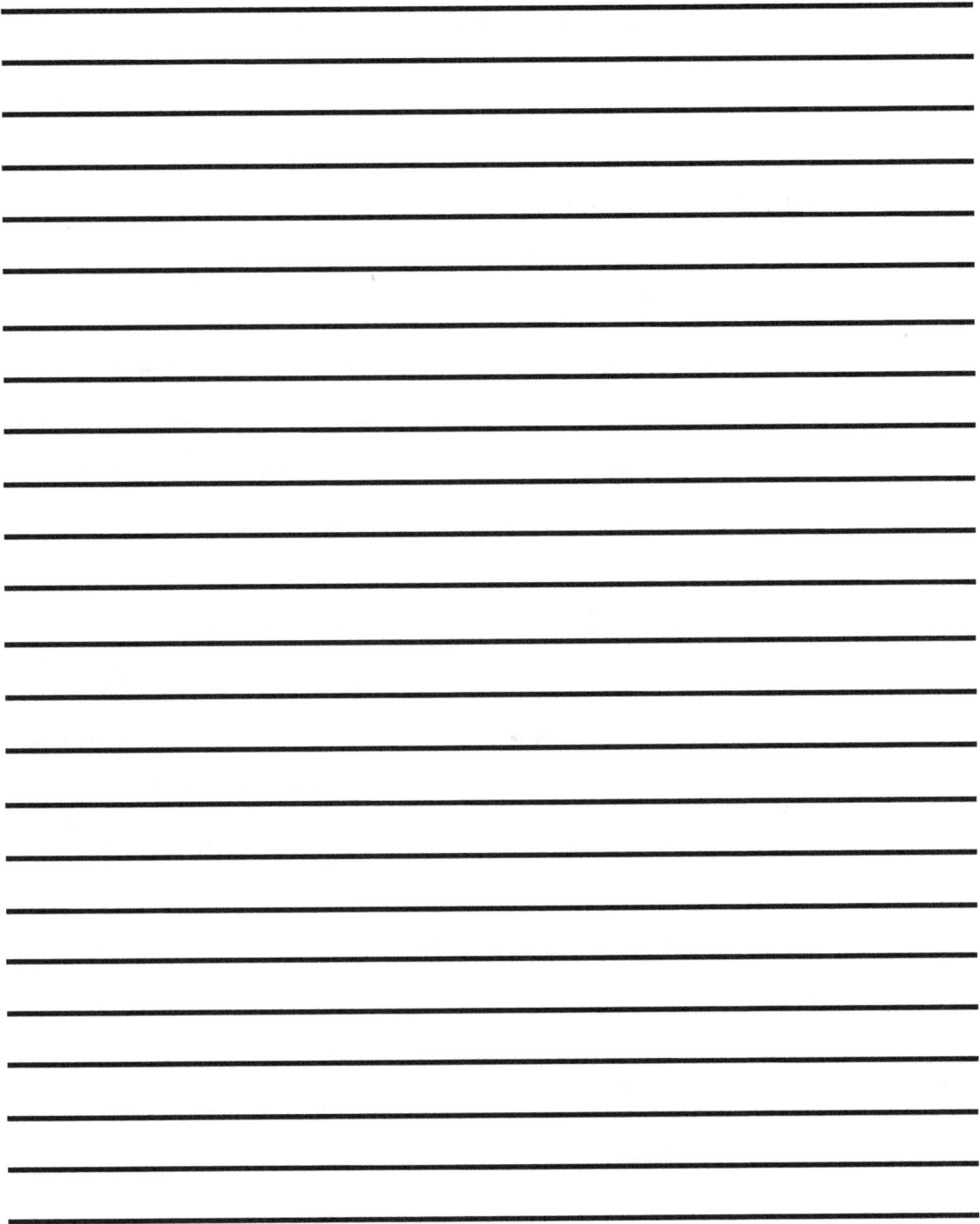

JOURNAL QUESTION 8

If you could talk to your birth parent(s) right now, what would you want to say to them?

Action: Write a letter to your birth parent(s).

_____

_____

_____

_____

_____

_____

_____

_____

_____

_____

_____

_____

_____

_____

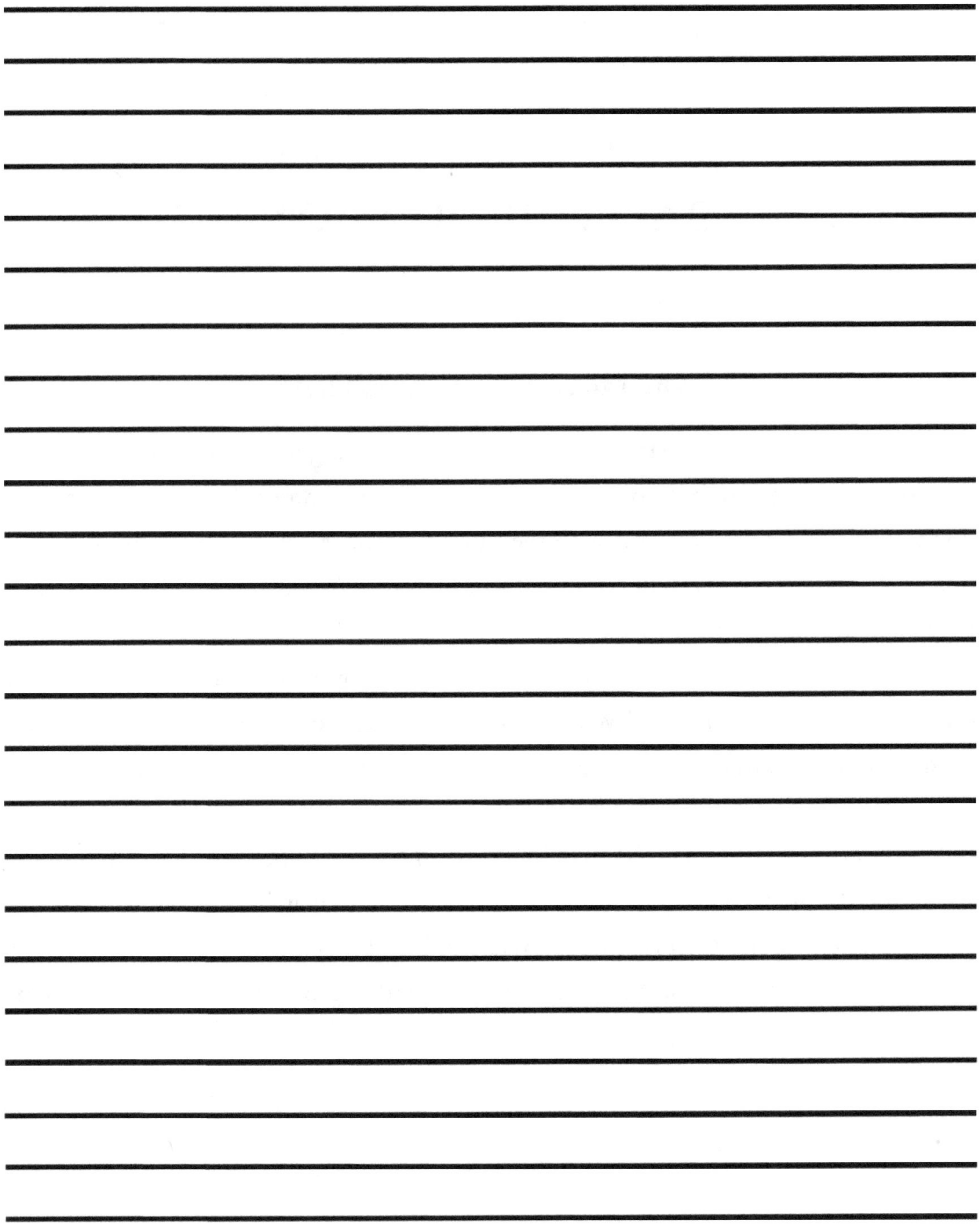

1

WHEN TO SEEK PROFESSIONAL HELP

When to seek professional help

Let's chat about this right up front. You may be reading this guide because you want to do the work of finding your birth parents on your own. Some choose this option because they don't want to trust someone else with their private lives. Many choose this because they don't believe they can afford the services of a professional. And others simply wish to learn how to do the work for themselves.

Each journey to finding birth parents is different. You will never know how easy or difficult the search will be until you get started. Here are some things to consider when making the decision whether or not to hire someone to help you.

1. A professional genetic genealogist or DNA/Adoption specialist will in most cases be able to complete your search very quickly. They may be able find answers in a matter of hours (best-case scenario) rather than the months or years it might take you on your own. How much money will you spend in those months or years working

on your own compared to the cost of paying a professional for a few hours of work?[1]

2. There is an emotional cost involved in drawing out a search over a longer period of time. Many people worry over who their parents will turn out to be or worry over what they will do once they are found. Getting answers more quickly will allow you to work through what *is* rather than what *might* be.

3. A professional genetic genealogist or DNA/Adoption specialist will have a great deal of experience in this kind of work. They will not only know how to deal with any situation that arises, but they will also be accurate. They will be willing to prove to you why their answers are correct. This sort of peace of mind is priceless.

4. If you wish to do some of the work yourself, a professional will work beside you and guide you. They will tailor the work to your needs.

5. I am often asked, "Why hire a professional when there are plenty of volunteer search angels available who work for free?" This is a good question. There are many search angels who may be willing to help you. But here's the catch. Often, those who are the best search angels and have a great deal of experience, have a very long waiting list—often months long. On the flip side, there are many search angels who don't have a great deal of experience or who can't provide the accuracy that should be foundational to this work. A professional will stand by their work. A search angel has no requirement to do so. Hiring a professional will give you immediate, high-quality service, with an accuracy that won't leave you wondering.

---

[1] **Cost Analysis** (these costs are estimated or correct at the time of publication): 6 month subscription to *Ancestry* with newspapers included $259.00 + *My Heritage* yearly subscription $299.00 + *Find My Past* $299.00 yearly subscription + *GenealogyBank* newspapers yearly subscription ~$99.00.
A friend shared these UK estimates with me: "I spent £225 for *My Heritage*, £177 for *Ancestry*, £170 for *Find my Past* and £200 for *Irish Ancestors* in one year."

A Genetic Genealogist will charge and average of $50 or £50 an hour and spend an average of ten billable hours on your search.

Who is Right For You?

Just like setting goals for your search journey, you should sit down and make a list of what abilities and traits are most important to you in a research professional. Is efficiency more important or kindness and caring? Do you want someone who has the time in their schedule to work on this quickly or would you prefer someone who is booked solid, but has a very high success rate?

Also, you need to set a budget ahead of time. There is no way to predict how long a search can take. Most professionals will contract a set amount of hours with you at the start and then add on additional hours as needed. If you have a couple of professionals in mind, get a quote on their hourly rate. Don't forget to ask about any extra costs that might be built in to the search. In the end, who you choose may be the person who better fits your budget.

To find a professional genetic genealogist who works with post adoption or unknown parentage cases, the best place to look is at the Association of Professional Genealogists website www.apgen.org. These are professional genealogists who have agreed to work at the highest standard of research. In other words, they use the Genealogy Standard of Proof. (https://bcgcertification.org/ethics/ethics-standards/#GPS)

Through the APG website you are more likely to get a professional who will back up their searches with solid evidence using primary sources. In order to be an APG member, they must also agree to follow the APG code of ethics. (https://www.apgen.org/code_of_ethics.php)

Although many professionals outside of the USA and Canada are members of APG, the number is not high. If you live outside of the USA and Canada, do an internet search for a similar organization for professional genealogists in your country or region.

To find a professional, go to the top of the APG website and look for the "Find a

Genealogist" button. Choose "DNA" and in the first dropdown and "Adoption/ Unknown Parentage" in the second dropdown that appears. The genealogists often say which state or country they live or work in. If there is no professional for your location, many will work remotely through video chats, email, and phone calls. If it is important to you, look for someone who specifically states they research in the area you or your birth family were born in or currently live in.

Once you find a couple of researchers to compare, look for customer reviews. This can tell you a lot about the type of person you would be working with. Ask for a consultation call with each of them to discover if they might be a good fit for your needs.

2

GATHERING CLUES

Now you have your goals written down. You've asked yourself the hard questions. The next step is to gather any available clues. This begins with your family. They are the people who would most likely have any information on your birth family if it was given to them at the time of your adoption.

Note: Before taking this step, make sure you have asked yourself question number four from the journaling section.

Interview your parents. Ask them anything they can remember from the time you were adopted. Every small detail can matter, so write them down in the Clues section at the end of this guide.

If you were adopted, ask these questions:

- Where was I adopted?
- Who handled the adoption? An agency, a lawyer, or someone else?
- Were you given any information about my birth parents?
- Were you given any papers from a caseworker?
- Do you have a copy of my original birth certificate from before my adoption? (This is rare, but sometimes is the case)
- Do you have a copy of the adoption paperwork?

If you are a donor child ask these questions:

- Were you given any information about the donor?

- Are there any rules in the donor contract that say I can't look for my birth parent? If so, what are they?

If you have one or more unknown or uncertain parent(s), ask these questions:

- Do you have any idea who my father (or mother) might be?

- Tell me about the time surrounding my conception. Where were you living? Who were you friends with?

A Note About Finding Paperwork for Adoptees

It is important to note that the paperwork available to adoptees not only differs by location, it changes over time as new laws are passed. Therefore, the best way to find out what is currently available to you is to do an internet search for your location. If you cannot find any answers online, try calling the department in your area that houses vital records (birth, marriage, and death) and asking how adoptees can obtain documents. If they don't know, they should know who to speak to. Usually records are housed at the county level in the USA and the UK, and at the province level in Canada. Some locations have documents housed by municipalities or parishes.

Original Birth Certificate

For adoptees: You will see the term original birth certificate used often in adoption circles. If you were adopted, this is not the same birth certificate issued to your adoptive parents after your adoption. Your adoptive parents' names will be listed as your parents on that birth certificate. An original birth certificate, OBC, is the document issued at your birth that should list your birth mother and sometimes lists your birth father.

Some states allow adoptees to obtain the OBC. Other states do not. Do an internet search for your state (or province or country) to find out if adoptees in your location can get a copy of their OBC and if so, what the process is. Apply for your OBC **today**. It can take weeks or even months in some cases to get the document, so don't put this off.

Caution: When birth fathers are listed on an OBC, they are sometimes incorrect. Either the birth mother listed the man she was married to or dating at the time, she simply was incorrect about who the father was, or in some cases she made up a name. This is why DNA is crucial to prove if the listed father is correct. More information about DNA will be provided in the next section.

For the USA, see the following resource to find a list of states with the current laws regarding access to adoption paperwork and OBCs:

https://adopteerightslaw.com/united-states-obc/

For all other cases of unknown parents

In some cases where one or more parents are not known, a birth certificate might give you clues, or even name one or both of your biological parents. This is a logical place to start. If you are not an adoptee, your birth certificate will be readily available to you, no matter where you live. Do an internet search for your state (or province or country) for how to obtain one.

Adoption Paperwork

Some states, provinces, or countries will allow adoptees access to their original adoption paperwork—also called their adoption file. It can have a great deal of information if it is available. Do an internet search for your location to see if adoptees can have access to this file and if so, how to obtain it.

If you have the name of the adoption agency, law office, or other organization that handled your adoption, make contact with them to find out if they will provide your adoption file.

Non-Identifying information

Non-identifying information is another common term you will see in adoption circles. This is information the adoption agency, lawyer, or government agency (depending on who handled the adoption) may provide to adoptees. It gives general information about your birth parent(s) such as their age at your birth, occupation, location of their birth, or family information. Sometimes it will contain information about you as a baby. It will not tell you the names of your birth parents nor give you enough clues to help you identify your birth parents directly. However, once you have narrowed down to possible birth parents using DNA, this non-identifying information can be extremely valuable in confirming you have the right person, or in many cases, tell you which of several siblings is your birth parent.

As with the original birth certificate, some states (or province or country) make this information available to adoptees and other states do not. Do an internet search to see if this type of information is available for the location where you were adopted and if so, what the process is. If it is available, apply **today**. It can take weeks or even months in some cases, so don't put this off.

Note: If you were born in one location (state, province, or country) and adopted in another, the non-identifying information will most likely be available for the location you were adopted, not the location you were born. Check both locations.

Adoption and Birth Family Registries

Adoption Registries

Adoption registries (sometimes called Reunion Registries) are websites where you can register as an adoptee looking for birth family. Birth families can register that they are looking for someone who was adopted away from the family. The hope is the two will be connected through these registries. Do they work? In some cases, yes. It's a long shot since both sides of the search have to be registered. But it's one more way to find your family and you don't want to miss out on the opportunity, especially the free sites. There are many registries out there, so try to sign up for more than one. Some USA state governments have their own adoption registries. Do an internet search to see what is available for the area where you were adopted.

Donor Family Registries

These registries are available to donor children looking for siblings from the same donor. Do an internet search to see what is currently available.

Note: Be careful. Some registries charge money, even legitimate ones. Make sure to read the fine print before joining. However, it may be worth paying money to join if the services they provide will be valuable to you. Do an internet search for reviews of the websites before joining or ask in adoption groups (such as DNA Detectives on Facebook) if you have a question about the legitimacy of a registry you are considering.

International adoptions

If you were born in a different country from the one you were raised in, you may have an additional layer of legal red tape between you and accessing adoption paperwork or an original birth certificate, which means it may be close to impossible. However, don't lose hope. A DNA test can help you overcome this hurdle. You may also want to consider hiring an international adoption attorney who specializes in your country of birth to advise you on what paperwork is available to you and how to obtain it. If you choose to go this route, do an internet search to find someone who specializes in adoptions in your country of birth, then search for reviews of their services before contacting them.

3

DNA TESTING

Even if you already have the name of one or both of your birth parents at the start, I still highly recommend you take a DNA test. This is the only way to ensure those names are accurate. It is not uncommon for names on a document to be incorrect or even falsified. It's not uncommon for a birth mother to give you the name of the birth father only to later find out the name was incorrect or the birth father was going by a false name.

A DNA test can also help you to accurately build your tree. For those who do not have the names of their birth parents, it will help you find your birth parents much more quickly. In many cases, DNA is the only way to identify birth family.

Who Should Test?

You have decided to get a DNA test done in order to assist your journey. Testing yourself is the obvious place to start, but who else should be tested?

- If you already know a birth parent or have identified a birth parent, ask them to test. This will help you when sorting your DNA matches as paternal versus maternal matches.
- If you can't get a birth parent to test, but have a biological half sibling, again, this will help you sort your DNA matches. A full sibling will not help you sort your

matches, but having additional siblings tested will give you more DNA matches. In some cases a person might not be a DNA match to you, but will match your sibling. This is the nature of how DNA is inherited.

- If you are not able to get a test for a parent or a sibling, but have a known birth grandparent, this will help as well in the same way. It is not quite as good as closer relative, but still helpful for sorting.

What if you don't know any of your biological family? This is okay. Your test alone is enough to get started. Later, we will talk about how to get more out of your DNA test results as well as targeted testing of additional people as you get closer to identifying your birth family.

Which Kind of Test?

There are three basic types of DNA tests available to consumers: Autosomal, Y-DNA, and Mitochondrial (MtDNA).

The Autosomal DNA Test

The autosomal DNA test looks at all 23 chromosomes of your DNA (22 chromosomes plus the X-chromosome) that are passed down to you from your birth parents, which were passed down to them by their parents, and so on. This test will give you ethnicity estimates which may give you additional clues. This is the best test to use for your search purposes and is the right place to start. It is also the most economical test.

The Y-DNA Test

The Y-chromosome is only passed down from father to son, so the Y-DNA test can only be taken by males. The results can be difficult to interpret and you may not get many matches since not as many people have taken the Y-DNA test yet. However, this is a good test to take if you are a male looking for a birth father and you have exhausted all other avenues of searching. It might give you a surname to work with. There are different levels of this test depending on how many markers (in common areas on the chromosome) you wish to have tested. The more markers tested, the more expensive the test. Currently, FTDNA is the only USA company who tests for Y-DNA.

The Mitochondrial DNA Test

Mitochondrial DNA (MtDNA) is passed down from a mother to both sons and daughters so anyone can take this test. However, it specifically follows the direct maternal line only. Again, the results can be difficult to interpret, but is a good test to take when looking for a birth mother and you have exhausted all other avenues of searching. It might give you additional clues. Differing from the Y-DNA test, there is only one level of MtDNA test. Currently, FTDNA is the only USA company who offers this test. Like the Y-DNA test, this test is more expensive than autosomal tests and may result in only a small number of matches who aren't very close in relationship.

Important Note: I never recommend taking a Y-DNA or mtDNA test at the beginning of a search unless you have a large budget. However, I do recommend them if you have exhausted all of the autosomal DNA matches from all of the DNA companies and still need additional clues. As more and more people take these specialized tests, more information becomes available.

Where To Test?

What I am getting ready to tell you is my opinion based on my personal experience helping adoptees and others to search for birth family. I will give options based on different scenarios, but when it comes down to it, you need to do what is best for you and your needs.

A Starting Place

The number one place I recommend you take a DNA test is Ancestry.com and here are some reasons why:

- Besides the fact that more than twenty-five million people have tested at Ancestry, their biggest draw is that many of their DNA matches have trees. And the trees at Ancestry are easy to read unlike other DNA testing companies who do not have user friendly trees. These trees will become a primary tool in your search.
- Once you have your DNA results from Ancestry, you can then upload your raw DNA for free to My Heritage, FTDNA, and Living DNA (as of spring 2025). This will essentially give you four for the price of one. Look in the Next Steps section for more information about uploading your DNA to these places.
- The price is comparable to the other testing companies and often goes on sale.
- Ancestry DNA is user friendly and they allow you to easily give viewing access to others who may be helping you in your search.

Adding On

After choosing your first test, you can do one of two things.

Option 1: You can wait for the results from the first test to come in, and see how many DNA matches you have and how close the relationships are. If you do not have enough matches to make immediate headway into your search, you can choose to take additional DNA tests. The reason for this is not only to get more DNA matches, but because you never know which company your birth family may have tested at.

Option 2: If you have the resources to do so, take more than one DNA test immediately so all of your results will come in at about the same time.

I recommend testing at these companies in this order:

Autosomal testing:

#1 Ancestry DNA
Note: you will need to pay for an Ancestry subscription by one month, six months, or yearly in order to access all the DNA features you will need. This includes seeing full trees. However, the money will be well spent due to the quality of those features.

#2 My Heritage
I do not recommend paying for a test here because the DNA tools will not be available to you for free and you will be required to pay for a yearly subscription after you test (they have no monthly option). Instead, upload your Ancestry DNA or 23andMe DNA test here for free. DNA tools are available for a one time unlock fee of about $29. I recommend paying the fee because you will not be able to see shared matches unless you do. (Note: as of June 2025, My Heritage began phasing out free uploads. You will need to check if this option is still available to you)

#3 23andMe

They do not accept uploads from other companies, but by paying for a test here, you may pick up additional DNA matches. Although you will get the needed shared DNA matches here, 23andMe is not a genealogy DNA website. This means their features for genealogical purposes will be limited.

#4 FTDNA (Family Tree DNA)

Upload here for free. They charge a one time unlock fee for DNA tools of about $19, but you may not need these tools, so hold off on paying the fee until you know for certain.

#5 Living DNA

This company caters to Northwest Europe, has fewer regions represented, and a smaller database of testers. However, I recommend uploading here for free to obtain possible additional matches, especially if you have any Northwest European DNA.

Y-DNA and mtDNA testing:

FTDNA is the only company who offers these tests. Hold off on buying either of these tests until you have worked with the Autosomal DNA first, unless you have a large budget.

Exceptions

If you live outside of the USA, some of the recommended companies above may not be available to you. In this case, you may not have a choice of where to test and will have to use what is available. In some countries, DNA testing for genealogy is illegal so this research tool will not be available to you.

Privacy Concerns

Many people are reticent about taking a DNA test because they fear the DNA companies will sell their DNA to other companies or will allow others access to their raw DNA. I am not a legal expert so I cannot fully address this topic, but what I do highly recommend is that before you click the "I Agree" button—read the terms of service for each company. I discovered when I registered my DNA test at one company, that I had to make sure I opted **out** of their program that would send my DNA to a third party for research. Taking a DNA test is a very serious step. Make sure to read **all** of the fine print to know and understand what each company does with your DNA. And if after reading you do not understand, call the company and ask questions.

Trusted DNA Companies For Family Research

- www.ancestry.com
- www.familytreedna.com
- www.23andme.com
- www.myheritage.com
- www.livingdna.com

How To Test

All of the major DNA companies will require one of two methods of giving a DNA sample —spitting or swabbing. For those using the spit method, you will be given a tube in which you will literally spit. For the swabbing method, you will be given what looks like a long q-tip in order to swab or wipe the inside of your cheeks.

Whichever method of DNA sampling your chosen DNA company requires there are a few steps that can help you assure your sample is a good one. If it is not, you may send in your sample only to find out six weeks later the company was unable to extract any DNA from it. The company then has to send another test kit and the process begins over again. This is frustrating and can add time to your search for family.

Here are some tips on how to send in the best sample possible.

Before you begin, wash your hands.

When you wake up in the morning, brush your teeth. Then wait one hour before giving your sample. In that hour, put absolutely nothing in your mouth. Do not eat, drink, smoke, chew gum or even kiss. Yes, I did say kiss. Kissing can involve the transference of DNA cells from one person to another which can affect your sample. Don't put anything on your lips such as medicated balms or lipstick.

If you are using the spit method, you now simply spit into the tube. Make sure you provide enough saliva—up to the recommended line on the tube—and make sure nothing but your saliva goes into the tube. Then follow the company's directions on how to seal the tube and send it off.

If you are swabbing, you will rub the inside of your cheek with the swab. Rub with about the same pressure you brush your teeth and do this for 30-45 seconds. Don't let the swab touch anything else before you put in into the container provided.

If for some reason, the company is unable to extract DNA from your sample, they will send another kit to you free of charge so you can try again. Sometimes, you can do everything right, but run into this problem.

!VERY VERY IMPORTANT!

!! Before you mail in your sample, make sure you have registered your sample ID number with the company online. There is no name on the sample so if you do not register it, the company will have no idea who the sample belongs to and they will throw it away when they receive it. Follow the instructions given in the test kit for how to register !!

Once you put your sample in the mail, the waiting game begins! I promise you will be on the edge of your seat in suspense as you wait, and if you are like me, you will check your status on the DNA website several times a week even though they will email you with updates. Take this time to complete your Journey Journal entries and gather additional clues.

4

GETTING READY TO BEGIN

You've completed your goals, asked yourself the hard questions, gathered all the available clues you can find, and sent off your DNA test kit. Before moving forward, there are some things you should set up so they will be available to you for the next leg of this journey.

Genealogy Websites

These are three genealogy websites I recommend you register for right now regardless of where you live.

Ancestry

If you took my advice and used Ancestry DNA for your first DNA test, you will already have registered there with a free account. If you haven't, go ahead and do it now. Ancestry has thousands of trees at your fingertips and you will want the ability to send messages to tree managers. Ancestry also offers some records with the free subscription. This is where you will want to build your DNA mirror trees because you can do it in private where no one can see them.

WikiTree

WikiTree.com is a one-world tree, which means every person who ever lived has one profile that is shared by all the descendants. This makes it a great place to collaborate with others and ask questions about ancestors. They have a forum called g2g where you can ask for research help if you get stuck. If you add your DNA test information to your profile, once you build a tree this information will populate through six generations of your tree so you can compare DNA test information with those potentially related to you. And best of all, WikiTree is 100% free. You will not get DNA matches here, but once you have some of your birth family tree information, you can get help extending that tree. It is also a great place to check for accurate family tree information when building mirror DNA trees.

Family Search

FamilySearch.org is also a one-world tree, but doesn't have the strong collaboration like WikiTree. However, what they do have is an amazing searchable database of billions of documents you can access for 100% free once you have registered. Ancestry and Family Search don't always have the same documents, so it's best to have access to both websites when doing research. If you can't find a document at one website, it might be at the other.

Other Free Websites

Geneanet

If you are outside of the USA, Geneanet may be a helpful place to find family tree information.

Find A Grave

Find A Grave has memorial pages for anyone who has passed away. You may find valuable information from headstones, connected family members, and any obituaries or other information that is posted.

FreeBMD

https://www.freebmd.org.uk is a free UK database that has records for the period of 1837-1997. If you live in the UK or have DNA matches in the UK, this is an extremely valuable resource.

Other Pay-to-Use Websites

Newspapers

If you have the budget, you might consider subscribing at least short term to one or both of the major newspaper websites. What they offer are obituaries and news articles that could be critical to your search. You can get Newspapers.com as part of your subscription to Ancestry, however this also comes with a Fold3 subscription which you might not want. In this case, check out the price comparison of getting the basic subscription at Ancestry and a separate Newspapers.com subscription. Genealogy Bank is another good newspaper website which offers an excellent searchable obituary database. Both Newspapers and Genealogy Bank have short-term free trial options so you can check out what they have available.

Public People Searching

Once you narrow your search down to possible birth family, you might want to look up contact information outside of social media. In this case, at least a short-term subscription to a people searching website such as BeenVerified can be helpful. Some of these websites allow you to pay per look up, but it can be pretty costly. Do some price comparing and see what works best for your needs. White Pages and Instant CheckMate are two other popular companies.

My Heritage

Some people prefer a My Heritage subscription over Ancestry. However, their payment plan is by year only. It may be a little less expensive than Ancestry, but you have no option to pay by the month or every six months. But if you know your family may have come from outside the USA, My Heritage has a growing collection of European records. Both Ancestry and My Heritage have a free short-term trial. I recommend trying them both and checking for yourself which one fits your needs and preferences.

Other genealogy websites

If you are outside the USA, you will likely want to consider some other genealogy websites that have more documents for your location. For those in the UK, Find My Past offers more in the way of UK documents as well as some newspapers. They have a free short-term trial option so you can see what they offer and if it meets your needs. Scotlands People offers documents for Scotland. They are a pay-per-download website so you can pay as you go. In Canada if you have Quebecois ancestry, you may wish to consider PRDH at www.prdh-igd.com or La France at https://www.genealogiequebec.com/en/lafrance.

Do an internet search to see what genealogy research websites are available for your location.

"The only impossible journey is the one you never begin."

—Tony Robbins

NEXT STEPS

The Next Steps on your search journey are:

1. Understand what a DNA centimorgan is.

2. Understand what a DNA match means to you.

3. Learn the features of the DNA website.

4. Learn the next steps to take with your DNA.

5. Learn how to sort your DNA matches into family groups.

6. Learn how to build a family tree using your DNA family groups.

Each of these steps is crucial to the success of your journey. Please don't skip any.

5

DNA—First Things First

I have my DNA Results. Now what?

I imagine you have been checking your progress bar at Ancestry DNA at least daily. Maybe even hourly. So when you finally get that email from Ancestry telling you your results are ready, you are exhilarated. Maybe even a little nervous.

Before we begin working with your DNA, here is a very important note: It is unlikely you will have a parent or sibling show up as a DNA match. This happens only in about 10-25% of the cases I have worked with, and usually it's a half sibling, not a parent. But don't worry if you don't have these close family matches at the start. There is a proven method of piecing together the DNA matches you have in such a way that it will build your biological family tree and point to your birth parents.

Now Let's Begin!

Note: as with all websites, Ancestry makes small or big changes to their layout each year. Although the layout may be slightly different from what's described below, the main features should still be available to you.

Let's walk through some of the things about your DNA you will want to look at first and discover what they mean. When you log in to Ancestry, if you aren't taken to your DNA home page first, go to the Ancestry menu and click on "Your DNA Results Summary" in the DNA tab.

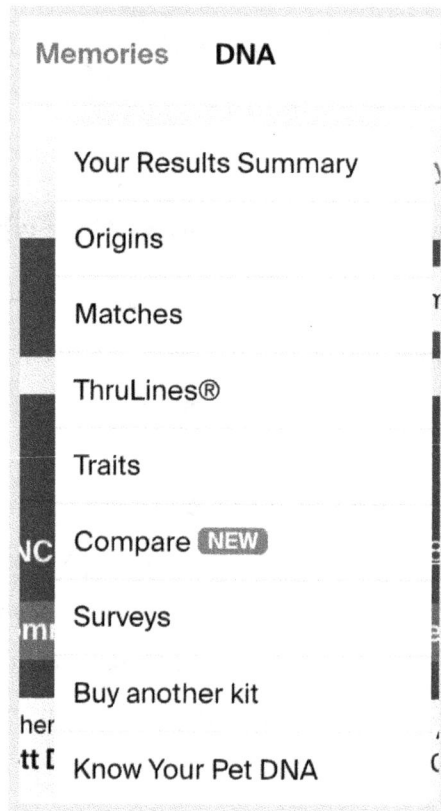

Memories **DNA**

Your Results Summary

Origins

Matches

ThruLines®

Traits

Compare NEW

Surveys

Buy another kit

Know Your Pet DNA

This takes you to your DNA home page. On the left will be a box showing ancestral regions (ethnicity), next are your ancestral journeys (communities), the next box takes you to your DNA matches, and on the right is a box showing your genetic traits. I know you're dying to see who your DNA matches are, so let's start there!

Click on the DNA Matches box. This will take you to your DNA match list. You will see your name across the top, then a DNA match menu bar below that. Below that is your list of matches. These are given to you in order of the amount of DNA they share with you. This is called a centimorgan or cM. The matches are also grouped by possible relationship to you—the closer ones listed first.

Note: Ancestry is only guessing your matches' relationship to you based on the amount of shared DNA. They are often incorrect on their guess. In one of my cases, a DNA match was listed as a brother for the adoptee. It turned out to be their uncle. Ignore these relationship guesses for now. The only exception is if they state someone is your parent or child. This will always be correct.

Let's Talk About Centimorgans (cM)

In simplified terms, a centimorgan (cM) is a unit of measurement for how much DNA you share with another person. The higher the cM, the closer the relationship. For instance, a parent will share about 3500cM with you. The lower the cM, the more possibilities of what that relationship could be. A person who shares 1500 cM with you has seven different possible relationships to you. However, a person sharing 500 cM with you has about fifteen different possible relationships to you. So how in the world do you figure out how the person is related to you? We'll get to that soon.

Centimorgan Auto Chart

Let me share one of my very favorite tools. If you go to https://dnapainter.com/tools/sharedcm,
it will take you to the Shared cM Project's auto chart.[2] You will see a box at the top where you can type in the amount of centimorgans you share with one of your DNA matches. It

---

[2] This page was created by Jonny Perl, creator of DNA Painter, but the numbers inside the boxes are from the Shared cM Project by Blaine Bettinger.

will then light up only the boxes that represent the possible relationships at that amount of cM. It's a wonderful visual way to see what those relationships look like on a family chart. Bookmark this web page for regular use.

On this chart, you will see half relationships on the left side. What does that mean? It means you are related to someone through half siblings. For instance, if my half brother has a son, genetically that son is my half-nephew.

How Helpful Are my DNA Matches?

Now let's look at your DNA matches and how much DNA they share with you. Your closest DNA match will be first. If you're lucky, you'll start with matches above 200 cM. 200 cM is about the 2nd to 3rd cousin range. Ideally, genetic genealogists like this relationship or closer to start with. If you see matches at 500cM and above, you have an even better start. These are in the 1st to 2nd cousin range.

How close are yours?

Now take a minute to read through the first several names on your DNA match list. These are all your cousins (or closer). These people are all a part of your biological family who have taken a DNA test.

If you already know one of your birth parents, do you see any familiar names?

Sorting Matches by Parent

Ancestry sorts matches into two groups—paternal and maternal. However, at the start they don't know which side is which. If you already know one of your birth parents, go to the tab at the top of the DNA match list called "By Parent" and click on it.

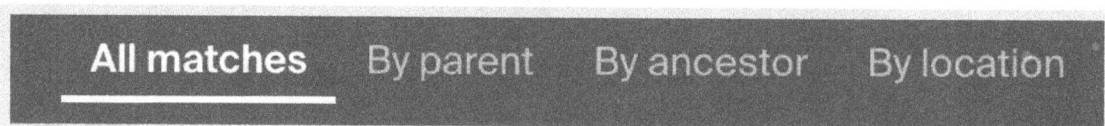

All matches   By parent   By ancestor   By location

Choose the group that you recognize as belonging to your known parent and set it as maternal or paternal as appropriate. This will automatically set the other group to the other parent.

If you don't know either of your parents, you will be unable to take advantage of this feature yet. However, your matches will be pre-sorted into two distinct DNA groups by parent.

Important Parts to a DNA match

It helps to understand all the website features available to you as you are working with your DNA matches. You will be using most if not all of these features in your search.

Note: Features differ from one DNA company to another. Spend some time clicking on all the buttons to see where they lead. I promise you can't break anything.

When looking at an Ancestry DNA match in the match list, going across from left to right you will see a photo (or photo circle), their name, their possible relationship to you and the amount of cM shared, then the number of people in their tree (or if there is no tree or an unlinked tree), a View Match button, and a + sign to add/edit DNA groups.

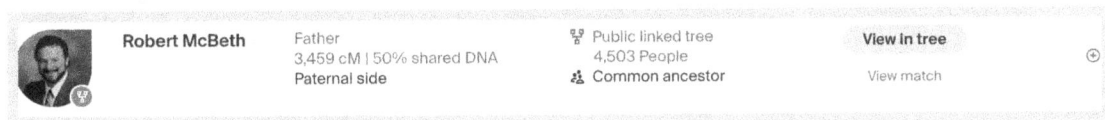

Robert McBeth	Father 3,459 cM | 50% shared DNA Paternal side	Public linked tree 4,503 People Common ancestor	**View in tree** View match

Clicking on their picture, name, or the number in their tree takes you to their DNA match profile. We'll look more at this in a moment.

Clicking on the amount of shared cM will tell you more about the possible relationships to you.

+Add/edit groups is something you will be using often when you start working with the DNA matches. We'll talk about that later.

Important Note About Privacy

This is a great time to stop and talk about the privacy of your DNA matches. I shared the above DNA match because he's my deceased father and I am the administrator of his DNA. I would never share anything about any DNA match (no matter how closely related) without their permission and you shouldn't either. Please don't post a list of your matches, the names of your matches, or any other identifying information about your matches anywhere. Not only does this go against the website's terms of service as well as privacy laws, it can also hurt potential relationships with matches.

DNA Match Profile

Now click on any match's name and let's look at their profile.

Note: I prefer to open each match in a new tab to the right. Right click on the link to do this. This will save you from constantly clicking the back button.

You will see some of the same things including their name, possible relationship, and amount of shared DNA. However, when you are in this view, when you click on their highlighted name, it will take you to their Ancestry account profile. This may give you additional information about the person. If they have additional family trees, you will see them listed there.

Below the amount of shared DNA on their profile, you will again see +add/edit groups. Next to that is an icon of a piece of paper and "Add Note." When you click on this, a window on the side will open up where you can add notes as you work. This is a valuable way to keep track of clues as you discover them.

Next you will see three tabs: Trees, Ethnicity, and Shared Matches. You will be using all three of these tabs regularly.

🔧 Tools ∨

You and Robert McBeth

🔀 **Father**

50% shared DNA: 3,459 cM across 26 segments

[View in tree]   [Message]   [Edit Relationship]

⊕ Add to group   ⊟ Add note

Trees   Ethnicity   Shared Matches

Below that, if they have a linked tree, you will see the first five generations of their tree. In order to see more, you need to click on the "Expand Tree" link. This will open their tree in another tab.

On the left of the tree is a Common Ancestors box. This information is only available if you have a tree linked to your DNA and if Ancestry has identified ancestors in common with the DNA match. This is called their ThruLines system. Be cautious when looking at ThruLines if you do have a linked tree. Those common ancestor hints are only as good as the genealogy in people's trees. If the genealogy is wrong, the ancestors are wrong.

The DNA Match View Menu

If you didn't open the DNA match profile in a new tab, click the back button. If you did, you can now close that tab.

Let's look at the menu at the top of the DNA match page. On the right you will see these options:

The first feature allows you to filter your matches in a myriad of ways. Click through each of the options to see what is available to you.

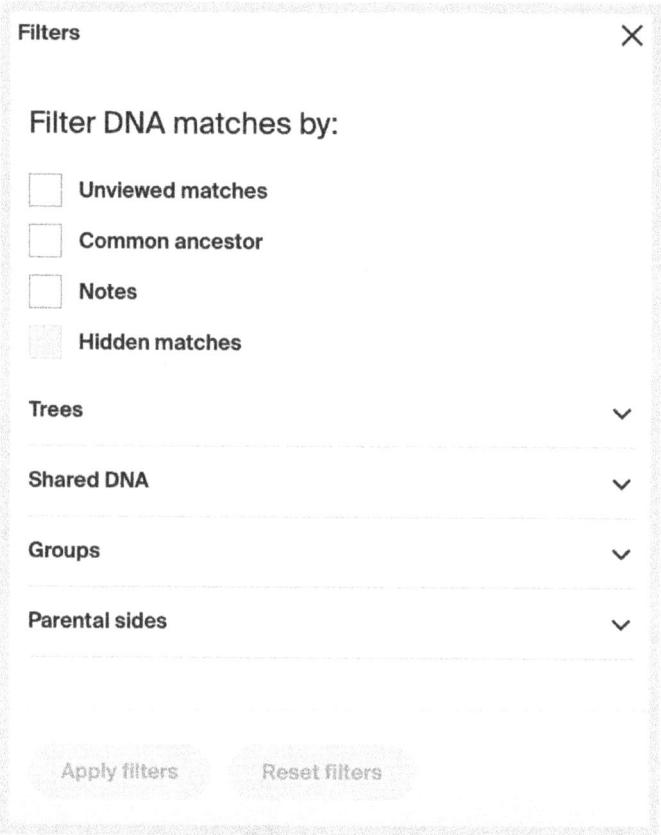

I will walk you through the process of creating groups soon. Each group will have a colored dot and whichever name you give it.

57

To the right of groups is your Search button and a Sort button. Click on the Search button and it will open a search window where you can search all DNA matches by the DNA match name, a surname, or a location in the tree. This is a very valuable tool.

Clicking on the Sort button will allow you to sort your DNA matches by the most recent. This is helpful if you wish to check regularly for new matches. They will appear at the top.

Ethnicity Estimates

Now that you've savored your DNA matches, let's hop on over to your ethnicity estimates to see what you have. Right below your name at the top of the DNA match list, choose the Origins tab.

Note: The keyword here is "estimate." This means the countries and percentages aren't precisely accurate. At times I have had Italian in my estimates instead of French. I've had Scottish that should have been English (and vice versa). Be careful in how you interpret the information. It's best to think of ethnicity in terms of regions rather than exact countries. See Your DNA Guide's Ethnicity Estimates
https://www.yourdnaguide.com/dna-ethnicity-estimates
for articles on how to better understand ethnicity results. Another thing to keep in mind is the DNA companies will change your ethnicity results as they update the science. Expect to see periodic changes in the percentages and even the countries of origins.

Some people call these estimates party favors because they are only good for party conversations. However, there can be some value in the information. For instance, I worked with a client whose mother was northwest European and whose father was 100% Italian. I was able to separate their DNA matches by ethnicity into maternal vs paternal buckets. Another client's father was African-American and their mother was northwest European. Again, it's easy to separate maternal versus paternal in a case like this.

A word of caution here. Ethnicity isn't always this exact. It's very common to have an African-American cousin who is related to you through your European mother. It's common to have someone who is mostly Italian related to you on your northwest European side. You have to be very careful and follow your DNA groups as your guide. We'll talk about how to create those groups soon.

Now that you've peeked at your ethnicity, let's move on to the next thing you need to do with your DNA before using the results to find your birth parents.

6

UPLOADING YOUR DNA

Upload Your DNA Everywhere You Can

Do you remember earlier when I said that buying a DNA test could give you four tests for the price of one? Now is the time to take advantage of that.

First, you need to download your raw DNA file from Ancestry. Go to your account icon in the upper right hand of the screen. Click on "Account Settings." On the left, choose DNA.

Click on your name under "Your DNA Tests" and scroll down to "Download or Delete." Choose "Download DNA data." Open that window and click the consent box. This will start the process. Ancestry will send you an email with download instructions. It is best to download this file to a desktop or laptop rather than a phone.

Note: Don't open the zip file of your DNA once it's downloaded! You will upload it as a zip file to the other companies.

Now let's go to each of the companies where you will be uploading this raw DNA. They are:

- **My Heritage**
- **FTDNA**
- **Living DNA**

Note: This list is current as of spring 2025, but may change at any time.

My Heritage

Go to https://www.myheritage.com/dna/upload This will take you to where you will both register and upload your raw DNA file. Within a few days (depending on how busy their system is), you will be given a match list just like at Ancestry. However, you will not be able to view the trees or shared matches unless you pay the unlock fee which is currently about $29. You may not need to pay the unlock fee unless you have matches above at least 100cM. You may wish to wait to see if you have enough information at Ancestry before paying the fee. (Note: as of June 2025, My Heritage began phasing out free uploads. You will need to check if this option is still available to you)

FTDNA

Go to https://www.familytreedna.com/autosomal-transfer This will take you to the link where you will both register and upload your raw DNA file. Within a few days (depending on how busy their system is), you will be given a match list just like at Ancestry. You will be given the matches for free and be able to view their trees. There is an unlock fee which is currently about $19 in order to make full use of their tools and features. You don't need to pay that fee until you know if you need their tools.

Living DNA

Go to https://livingdna.com/free-dna-upload This will take you to the link where you will both register and upload your raw DNA file. Within a few days (depending on how busy their system is), you will be given a match list just like at Ancestry. This company is still evolving, so the parameters of what you will receive and have access to may change. However, you should at least get your ethnicity estimates and a list of matches. If you have UK ancestry, this DNA company is especially interesting because they break your ethnicity estimates down by UK counties.

7

GROUPING YOUR DNA MATCHES

Now that you have taken care of first things first, it's time to begin working with your DNA matches. There is a way to group your DNA matches before even knowing how anyone is related to you. This grouping is important for the work you will be doing and will make more and more sense to you as you go along.

The Leeds Method

Although I taught myself how to group DNA matches through trial and error, my colleague, Dana Leeds, created a more refined method called the Leeds Method that is simple to use and has a high percentage of accuracy. See her website at www.danaleeds.com for more information. Ancestry has a colored dots grouping system that makes sorting matches using the Leeds Method very easy (My Heritage now has a similar dot system). I recommend using the colored dots, however if you prefer using paper and pencil or a spreadsheet over the dots, Dana Leeds shows you how to do that on her website.

In a perfect world, when grouping your DNA matches, you will have four DNA match groups—each one representing one of your four grandparents' family branches. However, this doesn't happen every time for several reasons. You might not have high enough DNA matches for four perfect groups, so you have to go to the next generation for groups. Since there are eight great grandparents, you could end up with eight DNA groups. In some cases, a great grandparent may have had more than one spouse so this group ends up split into two.

If you end up with more than four groups, don't panic. The work can still be done with ease. You will simply have more groups to process and possibly more generations to work with.

Sorting Your Matches Step One

Ignore all of your highest matches for now. This means anything over 400 cM. We're also going to keep a close eye on anything in the 300-400 cM range. I will explain more about this later.

Sorting Your Matches Step Two

Start with your highest match below 400cM. We'll call this match A. Remember that clicking on their name will take you to their DNA match profile. I always right click on their name and choose "open in a new tab" so I don't have to hit the back button. It also allows me to have multiple matches open at the same time when needed.

Click on Match A's Shared Match tab.

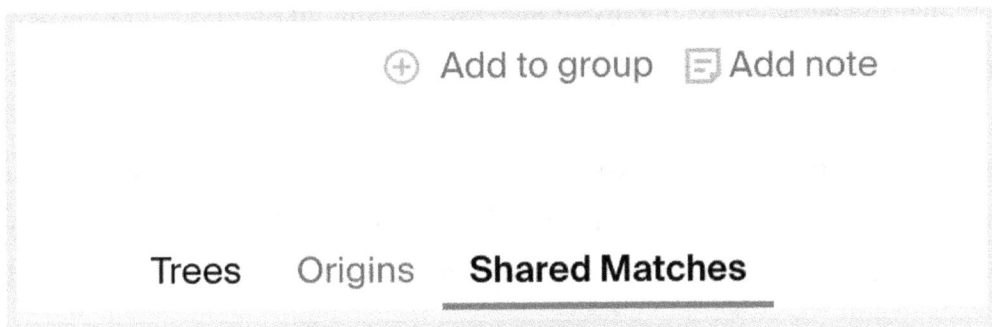

⊕ Add to group   🗐 Add note

Trees   Origins   **Shared Matches**

This shows you all the people that Match A and you have DNA in common with. Remember, this should represent the parents of one of your grandparents. This means Match A and every one of their shared matches are all related to you through this one couple.

Now, right below Match A's name click on +Add/edit groups. Choose +Create Custom Group.

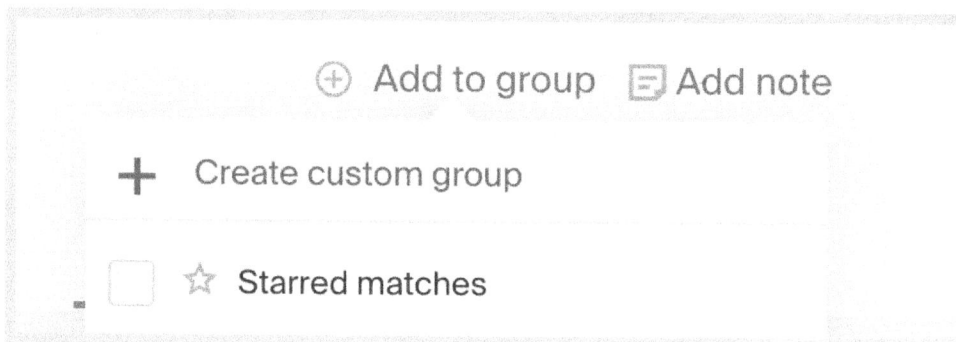

⊕ Add to group   ⊟ Add note

+ Create custom group

☐   ☆ Starred matches

We're going to call this **Group A**. Type the name in and click on the color bucket to choose a color for this group (or use the default color).

Next go to the shared matches and click on +Add/edit groups for your first shared match that has **fewer** cM than this match. On the right, choose the box for Group A. Do this for each and every one of the shared matches down to 40 cM. If this is a small match group with less than 20 matches, go ahead and mark them all.

Note: When grouping the matches into color dot groups like this, it's important to ignore any matches that are higher in cM than the match you are working with. Those higher matches may represent two different DNA groups. We'll find out later.

Sorting Your Matches Step Three

Close the tab for Match A and go back to your DNA match list. Hit the refresh button. This will populate the colored dot for all the matches you just marked so you will know they are in group A. You will now see that dot on the right side of the DNA match list for each match. Now choose the next highest match below 400cM who is **not** in Group A. We will call this Match B. Repeat the process. Open the match in a new tab. Click to add a new group. Call this **Group B**. Go to all the shared matches for Group B with a lower cM and mark them as Group B matches (ignore any matches with higher cM). Close that tab, go back to your shared match list and refresh again.

Note: In some cases you may see some people from Group A in Group B. Go ahead and mark them as Group B as well. They will now have two colored dots.

Sorting Your Matches Step Four

Repeat this process until you have placed all of your second and third cousins into a match group.

Sorting Your Matches Step Five

Now we'll revisit the highest matches we skipped during the Leeds Method. Go back to the top of your DNA match list and starting with the highest DNA match in the list, open their DNA profile in a new tab and look at the shared matches. Do you see one colored dot or two? Perhaps you see more than two. If you see more than one color of dot, this probably means you share more than one ancestor couple with them.

Go to each DNA match above 400cM you previously ignored, look at their shared matches, and add them to the DNA group(s) represented in their shared match list. (If you see orange and pink dots, add them to the orange and pink dot groups)

Troubleshooting

What if you notice many of your matches seem to be related to each other?

For instance, once match is in both Group A and Group C and another match is in Group A and Group D. If you are seeing quite a bit of this going on, it's likely that you have cousins who married cousins more than once in your tree. We call this endogamy or pedigree collapse. This can be a very difficult scenario to work with. If this happens, find a search angel or professional who is experienced in working with endogamy or closely related communities. They will have some tips and tricks on how to work through the difficulty of sorting your matches.

What if you have some very small DNA groups with only a couple of people in them?

This happens sometimes, especially when you have recent immigrants in your tree or family from countries that don't have a lot of DNA testing yet. This also can happen if there are just very few test takers from this family line. These groups can still be very valuable, however, so don't ignore them.

8

WORKING WITH YOUR DNA

Now that you have your DNA matches grouped, it's time to start using those groups to identify the key players in your family tree (also known as ancestors). It's important to work with only one group at a time so you don't get the groups mixed up.

Note: Another important thing to keep in mind during this step of the search process is the fact that your highest DNA matches will usually have the most valuable information. So we work with them first and look at them the most often.

Start with your highest match below 400cM (Match A) in **Group A** and open their DNA match profile. Click on their shared matches tab. If Match A has a tree, you won't be able to look at it at the same time as you are looking at the shared matches, so either open the "Expand Tree" link if they have a full tree or right click on the tab and choose "duplicate." This will allow you have one tab for their tree and one tab for their shared matches. Of course, if they don't have a tree, you can skip this step.

I recommend opening each shared match in a new tab so you can see the trees side by side and be able to go back and forth.

Look at the first shared DNA match's tree. Do they have any surnames in common with Match A? If so, you can add a note on their profile so you don't lose track. Keep opening new tabs with the next match in the list and so on. Look at the trees and compare them to each other. What surnames do they have in common? Hopefully, you will quickly see a common surname or two, or best of all, a common couple.

Not everyone will have trees, so only open tabs for the matches with trees. Some will have unlinked trees which means you have to click on the box on their DNA match profile to open their tree. This will open the tree in a new tab.

Start with the first five to ten matches. Keep all those tabs open for comparison.

Now that you've discovered some common surnames, go back to each match and look more closely. We don't just want common surnames, but we want the exact same couple in each tree.

Below is an imaginary example of what this might look like:

Match A (John Smith) shares 300 cM with you.

His paternal grandparents are John Smith and Julia Lackey. Their parents are William Smith/Dora Freeborn and Thomas Lackey/Mary Wentworth.

His maternal grandparents are Freeborn Ashford and Lovey Washington. Their parents are Moses Ashford/Henrietta Taylor and Lucas Washington/Bernice Green.

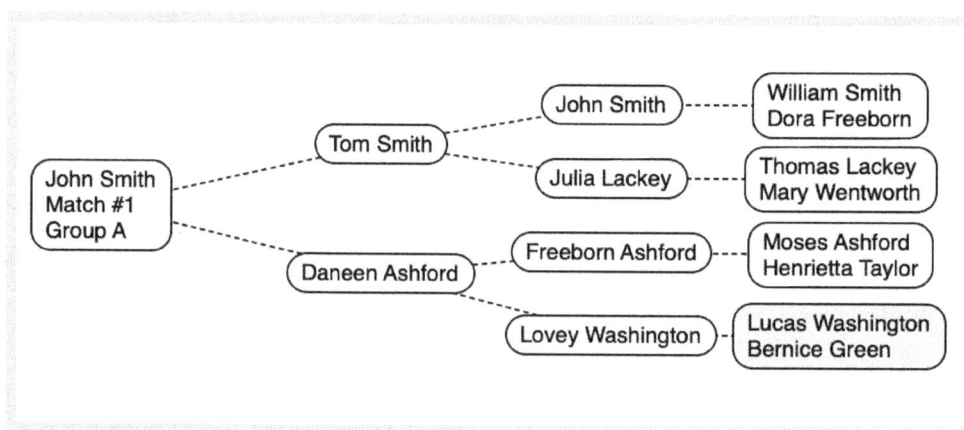

Shared match number one has no tree.

Shared match number two has Lucas Washington and Bernice Green in their tree.

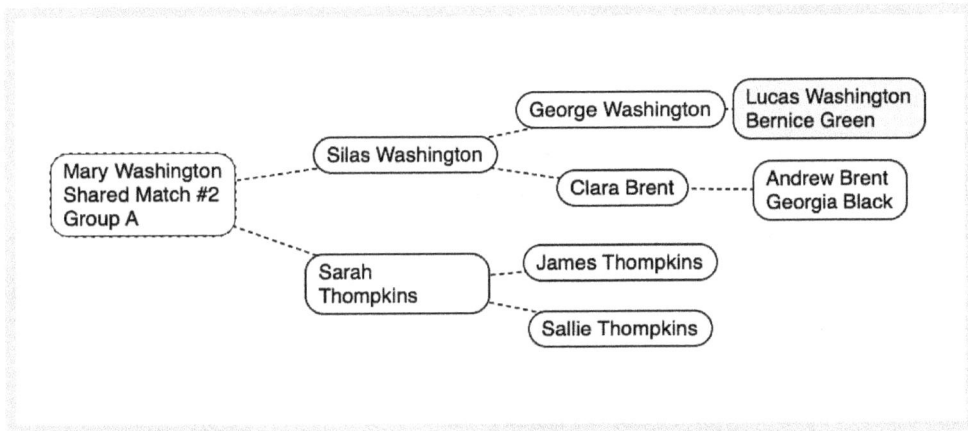

Shared match number three has a Washington, but you don't know if it's the same family yet. Come back later to explore this match further.

Shared match number four has a small tree, but when you build it out in a private Ancestry tree, you find Lucas Washington and Bernice Green in their tree.

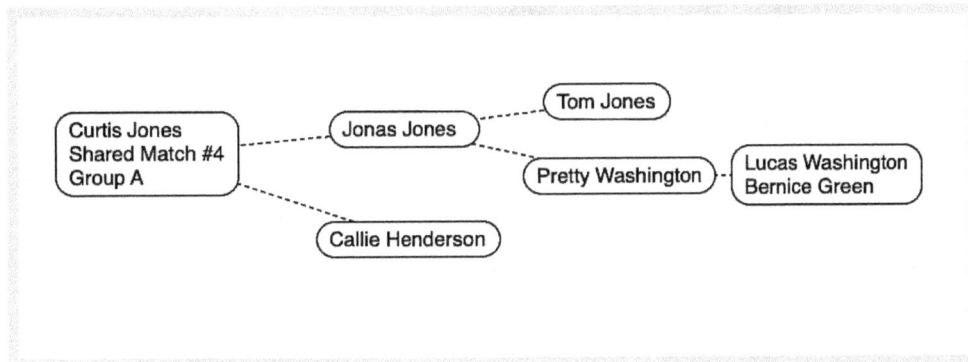

Shared match number five has a large tree, but nothing looks familiar. Ignore this match for now.

Shared match number six has no tree.

Shared match number seven has Bertie Washington and Annie Bright. You go back to Match A's tree and see these are the parents for Lucas Washington.

Let's stop here for a minute and assess what we're seeing. It looks like Lucas Washington and Bernice green might be the common couple for this group. However, you need to remember that how closely related a match is depends on the amount of shared cM. Go type in 300cM in the DNA Painter/Shared cM chart at https://dnapainter.com/tools/sharedcm. This will show you all the possible relationships at 300cM. I like to consider the closest relationships first. This match could be as close as a half first cousin. This means you would share grandparents with Match A or in this case Freeborn Ashford and Lovey Washington.

For this to be the case, we should see some relatives for Freeborn Ashford in several of the shared matches' trees.

Now go back to your shared match list for Group A and open more DNA matches in new tabs. Look at their trees. Are you continuing to only see family for Lucas Washington? Or do any family for Freeborn Ashford appear?

If you are only seeing family for Lucas Washington, then he and his wife are *most likely* our shared couple for this group. However, if you also see family for Freeborn Ashford, then Freeborn Ashford and Lovey Washington are *most likely* our shared couple.

Hopefully, you have added notes to each DNA match about which couple in their tree is shared with Match A. If not, go back and do that now. This is important information to keep track of.

Rinse and Repeat

Now go to all of the other DNA match groups and repeat the above process until you have a common couple for each group. You won't always be able to figure all the couples out at the start, but the more names you have to start with, the easier the next step will be.

Troubleshooting

What if your first match has only the parents and grandparents in their tree?

If this is the case, open a new tab and go to your ancestry account. Click on the Trees tab and choose "Create and Manage Trees." Start a new tree for your match. We call this a mirror tree. Set this tree to private in the tree settings. Add all the members from their tree to your tree. Once they are added, use documents provided for you by Ancestry (if you have a paid account) to build their tree out at least a couple more generations or until you find a common ancestor couple from that match group.

What if your first match has no tree or a locked tree?

From the DNA match profile view, click on their name and go to their Ancestry profile. Are there any open trees listed? If so, have a look at them and see if any have surnames in common with the shared matches. If not, send them a private message and ask if they will share their family tree information with you.

What if the tree has no surnames in common with other trees?

First, go to the expanded view of the tree. Click on the spouse or child for the DNA match. These will be private profiles, so you can't see names, but it might show if they have a tree. Often, a DNA match is the child or spouse of the person who created the tree and the home view of that tree is for the wrong person.

If that doesn't help, try searching the tree for the common surnames from that match group.

If these ideas don't give you any in-common family, this tree may be for an adopted person or someone with parents in the tree who aren't biological. You won't be able to use this tree in your work. But before giving up, send them a message and ask if they recognize the surname you've discovered from the match group.

What if only half a couple appears in some of the trees—For instance, Lucas Washington appears, but with another wife instead of Bernice Green?

If this is the case, just like we did with Freeborn Ashford, you need to check additional DNA matches for family of Bernice Green as well as the other wife. If family for Bernice appears in the trees, we know she is the wife for Lucas that you are related to. However, if the other wife's family appears in the trees, it's this wife you are related to. If you are related to Bernice Green, but a DNA match is related through Lucas and another wife, we call this a half relationship match since you are related through half siblings.

What if I can't find any common surnames or couples among any of the trees?

This happens sometimes. It might be due to the fact there is a lot of bad genealogy going on among the trees or it could be the trees aren't built out far enough. Start with the highest match and make sure it is built out at least four to six generations. For smaller matches, build at least six to eight generations. Sometimes you have to go even further for those smaller matches. If your top matches already have a good size tree, try building their tree for yourself, following the documents and sources. Very often people have the wrong ancestors in their tree without knowing it. These people more often than not have copied their tree from someone else without checking to see if the information was correct. Other times the names don't match because there are several NPEs in the trees. This means there is an unexpected biological parent or parents in the line where you share DNA with them.

9

BUILDING YOUR DNA TREE

Now that you have identified common ancestor couples for as many of your DNA match groups as possible, it's time to use that information to build your tree. Remember, these couples are your ancestors, so they will all fit into your tree somewhere. Figuring out exactly where is the next step.

Note: If you already know one side of your family, and you haven't already done so, start a family tree and build that side for at least a couple of generations.

Build a Mirror Tree

We're going to mirror what we know from your DNA match trees to begin building your own. Once you have more complete information, you will be able to transfer this to your partially built family tree, if you have one, or you can eventually turn this into your complete family tree.

We will start by using one couple at a time from your DNA match list. Use the common ancestor couple from **Match Group A**. Choose one of their children and create a new tree at Ancestry using that child as the first person in the tree.

How to Create a New Tree

Before you can add anyone to your mirror tree, you need to create a new tree. Go to the Ancestry "Trees" tab and choose "Create & Manage Trees."

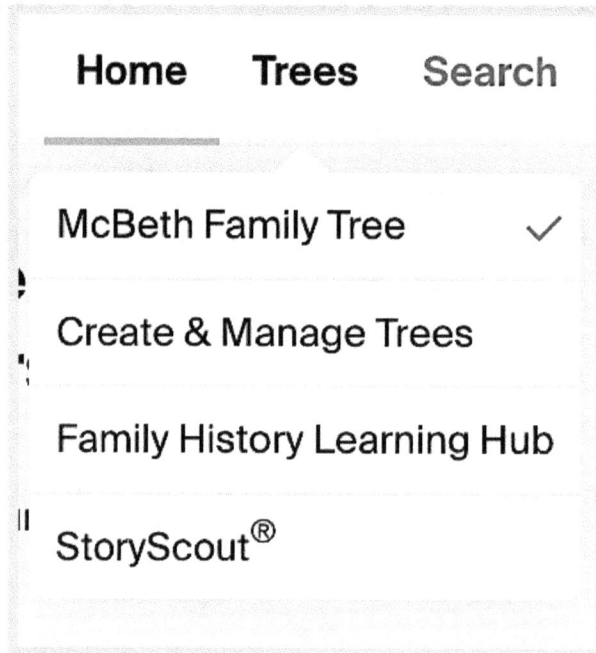

Home   **Trees**   Search

McBeth Family Tree   ✓

Create & Manage Trees

Family History Learning Hub

StoryScout®

Near the bottom of the next page you will see a link that says, "Create a New Tree."

⊹ Create a new tree   ⬆ Upload a GEDCOM file

Click on that link and add the child mentioned above as the first person. You will then be required to add one of the parents before you are asked to name the tree. For added privacy, you can name the tree something that won't identify what you're working on. However, if you're like me, and you will be building several trees over time, you may wish to choose a name you'll easily remember.

But First, Make Your Tree Private

Before you begin adding more family to this tree, it's important to make this tree private and unsearchable. Why? You will be doing some speculative work, meaning some of it may or may not be genealogically correct at first. You will also be working with relationships that are not yet known to your birth family. It's best to keep this private until you have had a chance to make contact with the family (if this is a step you are choosing).

To make a tree private and unsearchable, go to the vertical tree menu at the left of the tree. Click on the three dots. Choose "Tree Settings."

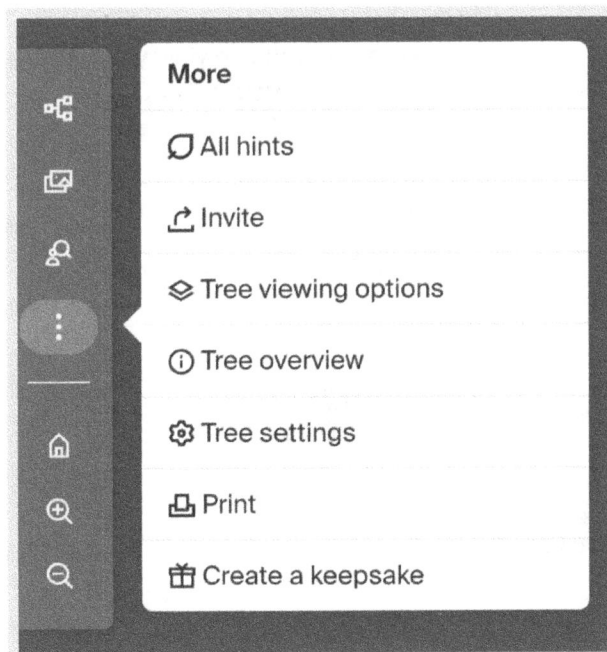

On the next page click on the Privacy Settings tab.

Tree settings

Tree Info   **Privacy Settings**   Invitations

Choose the Private Tree option, then scroll down and click the box next to: "Also prevent your tree from being found in searches." If you don't click this box, your tree will show up in Ancestry hints on the trees for others who share the same family.

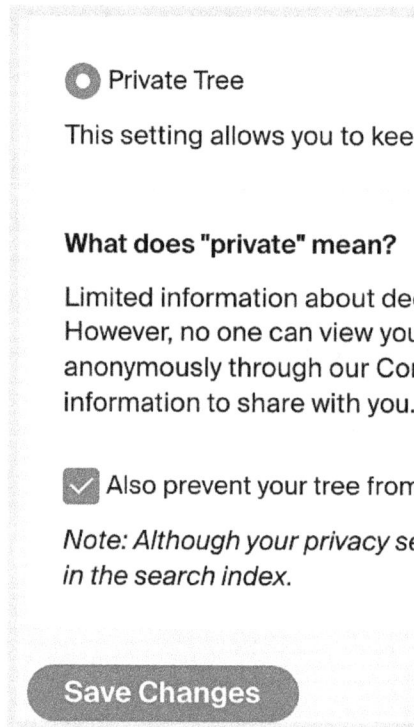

◉ Private Tree

This setting allows you to kee

What does "private" mean?

Limited information about de
However, no one can view you
anonymously through our Co
information to share with you.

☑ Also prevent your tree from

*Note: Although your privacy se
in the search index.*

Save Changes

Then click the Save Changes button.

One More Privacy Note Before You Begin

It is important to note that if you choose to add photos to your mirror tree from the Ancestry hints, people will be able to see that you added that photo and will see the name of the tree, even if the tree is private and unsearchable. Take this into consideration before adding photos from Ancestry to your tree.

Start With the Children

From our example, Lucas Washington and Bernice Green had eight children. One son was named John. I'm going to choose John to start the tree and add Lucas and Bernice as his parents. Once the tree is created, I'll open Lucas' profile and using sources, such as census, birth, and death records, as well as obituaries, I will add all the children I can find for Lucas and Bernice. One of the children may be your grandparent, depending on how closely related this couple is to you. It is important to discover the names of **every** child that lived past childhood.

I often will check the trees of other Ancestry members to make sure I didn't miss a child who wasn't enumerated in any of the census records. A birth parent of one of my clients was missed on multiple census records, but showed up in more than one obituary. This does happen on occasion.

Caution #1: Other trees may have children listed who are not children of Lucas and Bernice. Look for sources to prove any additional children are truly theirs.

Caution #2: Families often claimed grandchildren or other family members as their own children on records. Keep this in mind as you work.

Spouses and Children-of-Children Come Next

Now that we have all of Lucas and Bernice's children listed, we need to find out which of them is your next-in-line direct ancestor. The way to do that is to look at their spouses. The right child will have a spouse who is represented by another of your DNA match groups.

Start with the oldest child, go to his profile, and use sources to find the name of his spouse(s). It's important to find **all** the spouses for each child of Lucas and Bernice because you might be related to the second wife instead of the first. I like to add the surname of the spouse in the suffix field for each child. I add it in parentheses like this: (Jones) or (Jones/Danielson) if they have more than one spouse. This will give me a quick visual view of all the spouses' surnames when looking at the list of children from Lucas or Bernice's profile.

It might look something like this:

- John Washington (Dirkson)
- Pretty Washington (Jones)
- Titus Washington (Fielding/Carter/Smith)
- Samuel Washington (no spouse)
- George Washington (Brent)
- Amity Washington (died young)
- Verity Washington (Neal/Dunlap)
- Lovey Washington (Ashford)

The surnames of all of these spouses are mostly common names, but hopefully something will jump out at you based on the work you've already done to find common surnames and couples in the other DNA match groups.

In this case the surname Dunlap looks familiar to me since it's a common surname from DNA Match Group C. Verity Washington's second husband was Andrew Dunlap. To see if this matches the Dunlaps from Match Group C, I go to Andrew Dunlap's profile, and using sources, begin building his tree back in time, starting with his parents. In a best-case scenario, his parents will be the common couple from Match Group C. But often, you need to go a couple of generations back before hitting the common couple. Andrew's parents are Josiah Dunlap and Margaret Boyce. This is the common couple from Match Group C.

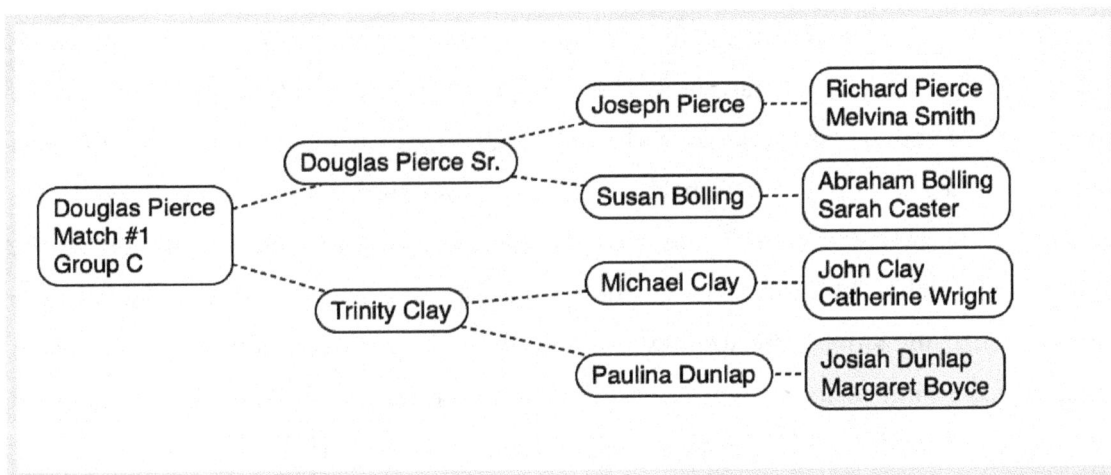

You may now cheer! You just made your first connection. We're going to double check our work in a little bit, but if correct, Verity Washington and Andrew Dunlap are your grandparents. This means one of their children is *most likely* your birth parent.

Troubleshooting

What if none of the spouses matches any of the surnames from the other DNA match groups?

There could be a few reasons for this. It could be because your birth parent or the birth grandparent was either adopted or born outside of a marriage. These cases are much more difficult to solve, especially in cases of adoption. I recommend you reach out to a professional or someone with a good deal of experience to help you on the next step if this happens.

However, it may also be situation where there is another marriage, but you haven't found it yet. This is fairly common. In these cases, I can often find the marriage by working with the other DNA match groups. Sometimes a marriage record will show up for one spouse, but not the other. If you still haven't found the marriage, keep looking. Also, try searching at FamilySearch.org. They have one of the best databases for marriage records.

Another reason why you might not find a common surname among the spouses is because you might be a generation off. This happens often. You may think you identified the correct shared ancestor couple in the DNA group, but it might actually be the next generation farther or a generation closer. If you don't find common surnames, **add** a generation to the tree for both halves of the common ancestor couple and add all the children for each side. Now look for the spouses of those children. If you don't find a common surname among the spouses, come back to the common couple and go **down** another generation. In other words, you already found all the children of the identified couple. Now find the children of all of their children and look at their spouses.

If you still can't find the common surname, come back to it after working with other DNA groups, or find a professional or experienced researcher who can help you.

Check Your Work 1

It's vitally important to make sure your work is accurate as you make connections. One way to do that is to double check the children of the other DNA match group couple. In this case, Andrew's parents are Josiah Dunlap and Margaret Boyce. You will want to find all the children for Josiah and Margaret and find their spouses. Why? It is very common for two siblings from one family to marry two siblings from another family. You need to double check that none of Andrew's siblings married any of Lucas Washington's other children. If they didn't, you can be pretty certain you have the right grandparents identified based on the two DNA match groups connecting through marriage. However, if you do find a marriage between a sibling of Andrew's and a sibling of Verity's, you need to keep in mind that at this stage of the work the other couple could have an equal chance of being your grandparents.

Finding Your Birth Parent

If you were fortunate enough to have two distinct DNA groups for this first side of your family, then finding your birth parent is now a matter of finding all the children of your grandparents and looking at them. Often there will be multiple children, so you will need to use any clues you gathered at the beginning of your journey to help you know which one is the right one. If you have non-identifying information from your adoption record, this may tell you the age of the birth parent and location of their birth. It might tell you how many siblings they had. If you have your original birth certificate, you may have a name to work with. If you have any of this kind of information, compare it to the list of children of the proposed grandparents.

If you are looking for your birth father because you know who your birth mother is, you will only need to look at the sons of your grandparents. This helps narrow things down a bit. But if you are looking for both birth parents, and you have no clues to work with right now, put this parent aside for now. Repeating the process you just completed for this side of the family for the other DNA match groups may reveal additional information that will help you figure out whether you are looking for your birth father or birth mother on this side.

Check Your Work 2

Now that you know where the first two DNA match groups fit into your tree, it's time to adjust your tree and do some more checking. Choose any of the children of your potential grandparents to be your birth parent (it doesn't matter which one right now). Add yourself as their child.

Note: I can't stress enough that your tree should be private and unsearchable at this stage. Adding a parent who might not be your parent could be disturbing to the birth family if they see it, especially if it's incorrect.

We're going to change the home person in this tree to you. To do this, you need to go to the tree menu on the left side of your tree and click the three dots. Choose "Tree Settings." On the next page you will see "Your Home Person in This Tree" on the right. It should currently say John Washington (or whoever you started your tree with). Change this to your name and save. Make sure to click the box that says, "I have selected myself as the Home Person."

Home Person

Emmaline MacBeath

or Browse the list of everyone in your tree

☑ I have selected myself as the Home Person.

Select   or Cancel

This is important because this tells Ancestry to show you how each person in the tree is related to you as the home person.

Let's go back to the tree now. **Click on it from the Tree tab.**

You will now check your work in another way. Choose a few of your top DNA matches from each of the two DNA match groups in your tree. In our example, this would be Group A and Group C. One at a time, place that DNA match into your tree where they would fit. You will likely need to add additional people to go from the couple in your tree that you share to where the match fits into the tree. Once you create their profile, look at the relationship Ancestry says you share.

In our example, our top match was 300cM. I placed him into the tree and Ancestry says he is my first cousin once removed. Now go to the DNA Painter auto chart and place 300 into the box. Does 1C1R show up for 300cM? Yes it does. This means 300cM can definitely be a 1C1R. This relationship checks as *possible*.

Repeat this with a few other DNA matches to make sure their relationship is possible for the amount of DNA you share with them.

Troubleshooting 2

What if the DNA I share with a match doesn't match the relationship in my tree?
There could be a few reasons for this:

One, it's an anomaly. Meaning, the amount of DNA passed down to one of you (or both of you) from this family line wasn't as large as usual for this relationship. This happens sometimes.

Two, you might be a half relationship to them. This means there was an unexpected parentage situation somewhere in their tree on this family line and you don't share both halves of the ancestral couple with them.

Three, you have something incorrect with your tree. If you have only one person whose shared DNA doesn't match the relationship, this isn't as big a worry. However, if several people aren't matching the relationship, find a professional or an experienced researcher to help you sort it out.

Rinse and Repeat

Now that you've placed two DNA match groups into your tree, you're ready to work with the others. Start with the next DNA group in your list. In our example, DNA Match Group B is next. Add the common ancestor couple somewhere in your mirror tree or start a separate mirror tree for this side of the family.

If you have only four DNA match groups, mirror tree building will be a much easier and shorter process. However, if you have six or more match groups, you will need to build a mirror tree for each of those match groups, which will take longer and require more patience before you can make the connections between groups. Keep building up the tree, down the tree and sideways on the tree (adding spouses) until you find the connections.

10

CONTACTING DNA MATCHES

There will be times where a DNA match doesn't have a tree or has a private tree. You will want to send them a message and ask them for more information. For the first message, it's best to give them general information.

You can ask them if they have a tree you can view or in the case of private trees, if they would share that with you. If they won't share or don't have a full tree to share with you, you can ask them if they will tell you the names of their grandparents or great grandparents. These names may help you find how they are related to the DNA match group they belong to.

Example Messages

Here are a few example message to send to DNA matches for more information. The farther out the relationship is with the DNA match, the less information that is shared at the beginning. You can share more information as they respond to you based on your comfort level. Please don't send these messages until you have done the DNA work outlined in this guide first. Sending messages too early before you know more about your DNA match groups could prevent your matches from communicating with you.

Hello <name>, You are my DNA match and we share 157cM. I'm working on my paternal family tree using DNA and knowing how you are related to the <name> family would really help me. Would you be willing share your family tree information with me? <my name>

Hello <name>, You are my DNA match and we share 157cM. I'm working on my paternal family tree using DNA. You belong to a DNA group I am working with that has Lucas Washington and Bernice Green as the common ancestors. Can you tell me if this couple is in your tree or can you share your family tree with me? <my name>

Hello <name>, You are my DNA match and we share 800cM which means you are a close relative in the <name> family. I'd like to find out how we're related. Please contact me so I can share more information. <my name>

Hello <name>, You are my DNA match and we share 1676cM. Based on the DNA work I've done so far, I think you are my <add relationship>. I was adopted and would like to tell you more about my story with the goal of <add your goal> <my name>

You can see that each of these messages mentions your goal. DNA matches are much more receptive to sharing information when you tell them this. Simply asking them to share their private tree with you may send them running in the opposite direction since not everyone understands how the amount of DNA shared with them determines your relationship.

Respecting DNA Match Privacy

Some DNA matches will never respond to you or share family information for various reasons, one of them being privacy concerns. Unfortunately, there is nothing you can do in these cases and you must respect their desire for privacy. If you choose to ask another DNA match if they know that person, that's fine, but please remember to keep anything you learn about that person private. For example, don't post that person's name and information in a public tree or ask about that person publicly online.

FINAL STEPS

"Not all those who
wander are lost."

—J.R.R. Tolkien

11

JOURNEY CHECK IN

You've already done quite a bit of work. Pat yourself on the back for a job well done! Now it's time to pull out your journal and check in with yourself.

How are you doing?

Are you feeling anxious, excited, overwhelmed? Are you thinking: Let's do this! or Let's not do this? Do you need a break or are you feeling energized for the next leg of the journey? Do you need more help?

There are no wrong answers.

Some people need to take a break or several breaks throughout the journey because it can become emotionally overwhelming. It's perfectly okay to put the work to the side until you are ready to pick it up again. Your journey should take as much time as you need it to.

If you chose to do the work yourself, but you're beginning to feel overwhelmed by all the information you need to gather and the steps you need to take, it may be time to seek professional assistance.

Remember, no two journeys are the same. It's good to recognize what you need and take time out to care for those needs.

Action: Revisit Journal Question 2 and answer it again in your Journey Journal. **How do I feel about this journey?**

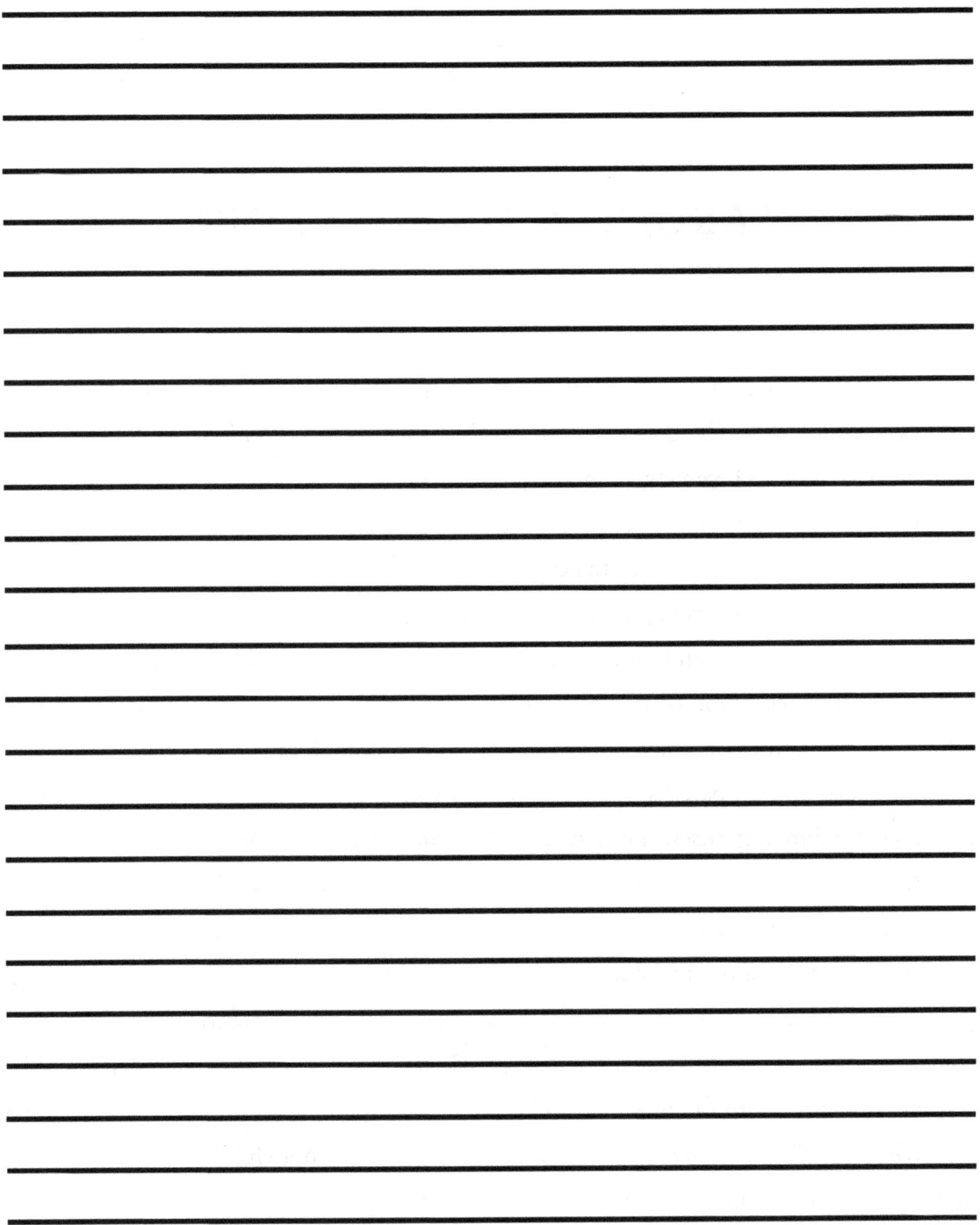

12

TARGETED DNA TESTING

Let's say you've done all the work with your DNA match groups and have built a mirror tree, but the pieces aren't coming together—the DNA match groups aren't connecting to each other. Maybe it's because you don't have close enough DNA matches (especially if you have little to nothing above the 200cM range).

Targeted testing can be a way to get you closer to your answer.

Going back to our example of Lucian Washington and Bernice Green, what if you didn't have a 300 cM match in this DNA group? What if your highest match was only 112 cM and the only common couple you could find were Lucian's grandparents? That's two additional generations of family in the tree you need to work through. If his grandparents had twelve children and his parents had 10 children, you could spend a lot of time creating profiles for children, spouses, children of children and so on before finding the connection.

As a solution, you could try targeted testing to get additional DNA matches.

This means finding other descendants of Lucian's grandparents to take a DNA test. It's important to find ones who are related through different children of this couple from your current DNA matches in order to get a variety of DNA information. Also, try to find someone who is closest to Lucian's grandparent's generation to take a test. This would be too far back in time for a child or possibly even a grandchild to be living, but if a great grandchild is still living, they would be the best choice. Then a child of one of the great grandchildren and so on would be the next best choice.

Another example where targeted testing might be helpful is if you can't figure out which child of Lucian and Bernice Washington is your grandparent because none of the spouses appear to match another DNA match group. You could begin the process of elimination by asking descendants of each of their children take a DNA test. If there are a lot of children, this could mean a lot of DNA tests and could become costly. But if you're willing to put in the time and money, it could be worth it in the end. Try to find someone who is closest to Lucian's and Bernice's generation to test. For instance, one of their children would be the closest. If none are living, have a child of those children take a test.

How Do You Get Someone to Take a DNA Test?

Getting someone to agree to take a DNA test is a little bit like cold calling. You will need to send the descendants a message, explain your situation, and ask if they would be willing to take a DNA test to help you with your search. The best place to start is by looking for trees at places like Ancestry and My Heritage that have been created by the descendants you are looking for and send them a message through that genealogy website. Usually, you will need to give them a little more information than you normally might to explain why their DNA test would be important to your search. Many people say no to DNA testing, but equally, many will say yes, especially if you're willing to pay for the test. When you offer to pay for a test, it is helpful for them to understand that you will not be in control of their DNA account. Once the DNA kit has been sent to them, you will see none of their information—only that they are a DNA match when the kit has been processed. The exception to this is if the person prefers for you to manage the DNA kit for them, but this is a much less common situation.

Another Example of Targeted Testing

Let's say you *have* been able to narrow down to possible grandparents or even a potential birth parent, and you're feeling pretty good about the accuracy, but you don't have close enough DNA matches to know for certain. In the example we have been using, 300cM is your highest match. This isn't high enough for final proof. You will need close family to test. The best choice would of course be the birth parent themselves, but if you are unable to get them to test, the next best choice is asking a potential half sibling, first cousin, or aunt/uncle to test. Even if their test comes back with a negative result (meaning they aren't the relationship you expected), their DNA match should provide additional valuable information. For instance, if the half sibling comes back as a first cousin match, it might tell you that you had the wrong sister marked as your birth mother.

Please see the Making Contact section ahead for ways to reach out to potential close family when you're this close to your birth parents in the DNA search. This needs to be handled more delicately than the case of reaching out to descendants who are not close family members as mentioned above.

13

BEFORE MAKING CONTACT

Things to Consider Before Making Contact with Birth Family

Once you have identified one or both of your birth parents, you may be eager to make contact. There are a couple of things to consider before you do so.

First, remember that you have been thinking about contacting your birth parent for some time, even before you had their name(s). But your birth parent has no idea you are about to show up on their radar. This will come as a surprise to them, especially for birth fathers who didn't even know they had fathered an unknown child. Take time to consider how your birth parent(s) might feel about the situation. Some will be elated since they had wished they could find you. Some birth parents will have negative emotions. This reunion may bring back up the emotions from difficult times before, during, and after your birth. Some will be in denial, especially at first. As you choose your words, think about how they will be received.

Next, remember that you have a right to know the identity of your birth family, but this doesn't include the right to a relationship. Your birth parent(s) may not wish to have any kind of relationship with you. This isn't about who you are as a person, but a choice they are making for their own personal reasons. This choice has to be respected. Trying to force any kind of relationship will not only hurt your birth parent, but in the end will hurt you. If you do want a relationship, but they aren't receptive, give them time to process everything. They may change their mind later.

If your birth parent refuses to even allow contact, again, this their personal choice. Step back and give them time to consider. They may allow contact at a later time. You might also try again after some time passes, but with a different family member.

Your birth parent may wish to keep in contact, but ask that their spouse or other children not know about you. This may make things more difficult, but it's important to respect their wishes.

Important Note

It is very important to keep in mind, if your birth parent or birth family rejects you in any way, **this is about them and their story**. It's not because of you and who you are. It's not because of anything you have done.

However, that doesn't mean it won't hurt. Consider working with a counselor to work through any pain this causes if this happens.

Publicizing the Relationship

First and foremost, before you publicize your relationship with your newly found birth parent, **make certain the relationship is confirmed by DNA**. See the Targeted Testing section regarding how to prove a relationship. In a few cases, there will be other proof of parentage such as a birth mother who secretly kept a copy of the hospital birth certificate or an aunt who was there at your birth. But I caution you: **don't skip this step**. You don't want to have to backtrack later and try to undo any pain caused if you find out you had the wrong person identified as your birth parent.

Next, when you have a DNA confirmation, consider the privacy of your birth family and how much they may or may not wish you to post publicly on social media or in a family tree. It's best to get their permission before posting anything about the relationship.

They may have other family who they don't want to know about the relationship yet.

If your family doesn't wish you to publicly acknowledge the relationship, what should you do?

This is tricky. Technically, if you have the proof, you should be able to post what you wish to about the relationship as long as the information isn't hurtful to your birth parent(s). But you need to stop and consider if you truly want to go against their wishes. How does this make you feel? Ultimately, the choice is up to you.

Can someone legally keep you from posting about the relationship publicly?

I'm not a legal expert, so cannot advise you on this question. Laws vary by location. It's best to reach out to someone who is a legal expert if this ever becomes an issue for you.

14

CONTACTING BIRTH FAMILY

One of the best ways to make contact with your birth parents or close family members is to first make contact with close DNA matches and begin a positive conversation with them about your search. They may very likely be able to connect you with the birth parent or other close family members. However, if you don't have a close enough DNA match or any matches willing to help you with this, you will need to make the initial contact yourself.

The next best way to make contact is through a certified letter. In a letter, you will have room to explain who you are, why you are searching, and what facts brought you to believe they are your birth parent. Always add your goal as one of the first parts of your letter to help alleviate any fears that you may want something from them that they aren't willing to give. Keep your initial goal simple—"I am looking for confirmation that you are my birth parent" or "I am hoping for health information."

By sending a certified letter, you will receive confirmation that the birth parent themselves received it.

Keep in mind that there is no right or wrong answer as to whether you should send a short general letter or a long detailed letter. Do what is most comfortable for you. The following examples are just to give you a couple ideas. You can write something completely different.

Example Short Close-Family/Birth Parent Letter

If you choose to use this template, change the information as needed to apply to your situation.

Dear <name>,

I have been searching for my birth (father/mother) and through DNA have discovered that I may be closely related to you since we share the same (maternal/ paternal) grandparents <add their names>.

I was born in <add location> on <date> to <known parent if known>. My birth name was <name if known> and I was adopted <date and location>. My name was then changed to <name>.

I am reaching out to you with the hope that we can talk about our shared family <or add other goal here>.

My email is <email> and my phone number is <phone number>. Please contact me at any time.

Sincerely,
<my name>

Example Long Close-Family/Birth Parent Letter

If you choose to use this template, change the information as needed to apply to your situation.

Dear <name>,

I wasn't sure how to approach you, but it was suggested that writing a letter may be the most comfortable way for people to make first contact with this kind of news.

For the past <timeframe> I have been searching for my birth [father/mother] and my search has led me to you. I was born <date> in <location>. My birth name was <name if known> and I was adopted <date and location>. My name was then changed to <name>.

<Describe here why you chose to search for your biological family>

I believe from the information that I have gathered <you can add here any specifics> and through the use of DNA testing, that your <father/mother> <or you are> is my birth <father/mother>.

<optional> I have enclosed some pictures of me at various ages in my life.

I know this letter may be upsetting because <you may not know about me or it may bring up upsetting circumstances, etc>, but it is very important to me that <add goal>.

I am willing to pay for any DNA testing that you will agree to do that will scientifically confirm my DNA research results. I look forward to speaking with you about all of this.

My email is <email> and my phone number is <phone number>. Please contact me at any time.

Sincerely,
<my name>

Reunion Services

Another way to make contact is to use a reunion service. These are people who are experienced in making contact on your behalf and setting up a reunion experience with your birth parents or close family members.

Do an internet search for adoptee reunion services in your location. Many of these charge fees for their services. Make sure to ask about that up front if it isn't spelled out on their website.

15

Finding Closure

Finding the names of your birth parents is not the end of the story. There are often many things that follow, depending on how you have chosen to end your search. These might include:

- Building a public biological family tree
- Meeting your birth parents
- Meeting other family members
- Sharing stories about your lives
- Processing past trauma

Since you have already done the prep work by asking yourself the hard questions, you know what you wanted from this search for your birth parent(s). Now that you have discovered who your birth parents are, what will help bring emotional closure? What do you need to make you feel like your search journey has come to an end?

Action: Answer this question in your Journey Journal - **What will closure to this journey look like for me?**

SPECIAL TOPICS

Donor Children

If you are a donor child (sperm or egg), your situation will be a little bit different from an adoptee's. You won't have an original birth certificate possibly naming the birth father and you won't have adoption paperwork. However, the donation center likely provided your parent with some non-identifying information about the donor. This may include physical characteristics, ethnicity, age, occupation, or some basic family information. Having this information will help you once you narrow your tree down to the great grandparent or grandparent level.

You also need to know that your parent signed some sort of contract when accepting the donation. These contracts vary by company and local law. Some contracts state that your parent will not attempt to identify the donor. Some state that your parent will not attempt to identify the donor before you turn eighteen. Please ask your parent about the contract and read it if possible. You don't want to get yourself or your parent in a sticky situation by violating any terms of that contract during your search journey.

Special Privacy Considerations

When a donor donates, in most cases they do it with the idea they will never be identified. They don't expect to have a relationship with the child (or children). But as more and more DNA tests are being taken by people around the world, this is changing the outcomes in cases of donation. DNA makes it easy to identify the donor. Some donors don't mind being contacted. However, as with all cases of unknown parentage, not all donors will want a relationship. Also keep in mind that a donor may have more children than (s)he ever imagined. This can be overwhelming. You have a right to know who your biological family is, but that right doesn't come with an automatic relationship. Keep your birth parent's side of the story in mind if you choose to make contact.

Other Unknown Parent Situations

(NPEs, MPEs, Foundlings, Foster Children and others)

NPEs/MPEs

An NPE (also called MPE) is the abbreviation for Non Paternal Event (or Misattributed Paternal Event or Misattributed Parentage). Typically this means the father isn't who everyone thinks he is. This could happen when a child is born from his mother's previous marriage, but the next spouse adopts that child. This could happen when a child is conceived outside of marriage from one man, but the mother soon after (or before the birth) marries a man who is not the father. This can also happen due to an extramarital affair or an outside of marriage relationship. Usually NPEs are discovered when a person takes a DNA test and discovers they have no genetic relationship to their known father. But they can also be discovered when a family member discloses the information. Although NPEs are usually about the father, they can also be about the mother. A person may grow up with someone who they believe to be their birth mother and later find out she's not.

NPEs will most often not have the correct parent on their birth certificate, but occasionally will. If you don't have a copy of your birth certificate, send for one.

Although family members might know the true identity of your unknown parent, the best and most accurate way to discover your true parentage is to use DNA. Family members might think they know the correct parent, but only DNA can tell you for certain.

Foundlings

Foundlings rarely happen in more modern times. Once upon a time, it was common to leave a child on the doorstep of the local church or orphanage. Today the police would get involved and work to identify the parent(s) immediately. That said, there are still foundlings looking for birth parents. In these cases, an original birth certificate is unlikely to be helpful since no identifying information would have been left with you. DNA will be your only option.

Foster Children

Foster children may have the names of their parents and even a birth certificate. However, finding the parents may not be a simple internet look up. A DNA test will help lead you to your birth parents and the birth family. A DNA test will also confirm if your known parents are accurate.

Other Cases of Unknown Parentage

If you were raised by a family member (your grandmother for instance), but you want to confirm your mother or father, a DNA test is your best choice.

Unusual DNA Situations

Endogamy and Pedigree Collapse

I mentioned this earlier in this guide, but it's a common enough occurrence that it deserves another mention. It's also extremely important that you understand how endogamy/pedigree collapse (cousins marrying cousins) can affect the amount of DNA you share with your matches. If there is a large amount of endogamy, it will throw everything off and you will think your matches are closer than they actually are.

Here's an example:

You share 650cM with a match. This appears to be a close family member (1st cousin, great uncle, grand nephew, etc), but in reality this person could be related to you twice— once as a 1st cousin once removed (about 429 cM) and once as a second cousin.

How do you know if you have endogamy in your DNA?

- The first clue is your DNA matches will all appear to be related to each other with no clearly defined DNA groups.
- Another clue might be if you have a very large amount of high DNA matches (over 100cM).
- Also, when you are building your mirror trees and the relationships and amount of shared DNA aren't adding up, this could be due to some endogamy.

Again, seek experienced help if you find endogamy in your DNA.

Less Common Unusual Situations

The following are less common situations, but do happen on occasion, so it's important to know about them.

Bone Marrow and Stem Cell Transplants

What if you have a birth parent show up as a DNA match, but they swear up and down that they were never a sperm or egg donor, never visited the location you were conceived, or never knew your other parent? They swear there's no way they could be your parent. Ask them if they have ever received a bone marrow or stem cell transplant. A person who receives a transplant can end up having DNA from the donor in their body. Transplant recipients are not supposed to take genealogy DNA tests, but it does happen. When it does, it could look like the recipient is the birth parent when in fact it is the donor.

On the flip side, if you have ever received a transplant, you should not take a genealogy DNA test. However, if you have a child, they can take the DNA test and with their permission, you can use their results to find your birth parents.

Identical Twins

Because identical twins pretty much have identical DNA, you will not be able to distinguish which is your birth parent using standard genealogy DNA or paternity tests. There are specialized tests that can be run if both twins are still living. Consult a DNA expert or genetic genealogist familiar with this kind of testing if you need to verify which sibling in a set of twins is your birth parent.

Resources

Trusted DNA Companies with DNA matches

- www.ancestry.com
- www.23andme.com
- www.myheritage.com
- www.familytreedna.com
- www.livingdna.com

Genealogy and Research Websites

General

- **Ancestry.com** Free to build a basic tree with registration, but you must pay for almost all of their features. Monthly, 6-month, or yearly subscriptions are available.
- **EnGeneanet.org** Free website where members share family information and resources. This is a European-based website, so if you have recent immigration in your biological family, it could help you build your trees.
- **FamilySearch.org** Billions of free family research documents (free with registration).
- **MyHeritage.com** Free to build a basic tree with registration, but you must pay for almost all of their features just like Ancestry. Only yearly subscriptions are available.
- **WikiTree.com** For tree building and research assistance (free with registration).
- **GenealogyBank.com** Newspapers (Subscription)
- **Newspapers.com** Newspapers (Subscription)

UK

- **Freebmd.org.uk/** Free Birth, Marriage, and Death record indexes for England and Wales 1837-1997.
- **Irelandxo.com** Free help with connecting to Irish ancestors
- **FindMyPast.com** Especially good for UK research. (Subscription)
- **Scotlandspeople.gov.uk** Search Scottish records and archives for free with log in. Pay per document to view.

Registries

Because websites change over time, please check each of these registries carefully before signing up to make certain they meet your needs, are private, and don't cost you money.

- **https://donorsiblingregistry.com/** For Donor children
- **https://www.findmyfamily.org/**
- **http://www.isrr.org/**

DNA Tools

- **DNAPainter.com** DNA Painter Advanced DNA tools
- **https://dnapainter.com/tools/sharedcm** cM auto chart
- **https://www.danaleeds.com** Learn more about how to use the Leeds Method.

Books

The Family Tree Guide to DNA Testing and Genetic Genealogy by Blaine Bettinger. A more in-depth look at DNA and how to use it for family research.

Blogs

https://www.yourdnaguide.com/ by Diahan Southard. She also offers DNA classes for all levels.

Videos

- https://www.familysearch.org/en/rootstech/session/you-can-do-the-dna-2-get-your-best-ethnicity-estimate for a video by Diahan Southard for how to better understand your ethnicity results
- https://www.familysearch.org/en/rootstech/session/the-leeds-method-grouping-dna-matches-to-identify-shared-ancestors for a video by Dana Leeds about the Leeds Method
- https://www.youtube.com/watch?v=MOHhxZN_GHA Crista Cowan, More Tips for Identifying Biological Family at Ancestry
- https://www.youtube.com/watch?v=UmOZXCxsqNU Building Quick and Dirty Trees (aka Mirror Trees) to Identify Genetic Matches by Blaine Bettinger.

Support

- https://www.facebook.com/groups/DNADetectives DNA Detectives at Facebook. A great place to find advice on using DNA to find your birth parents.
- https://www.facebook.com/NPEFriendsFellowship/ For NPEs

Other

https://www.gov.uk/adoption-records Accessing your adoption records in the UK

Using WikiTree as a Resource

Help Identifying Parents and Other Family

WikiTree has some powerful DNA tools that can assist members build their family tree. These same tools can help adoptees and others looking for their birth parents, or other unknown parents within their tree.

When you become a member of WikiTree, one of the first things you are able to do is to list on your WikiTree profile all of the DNA tests you have taken. This can be done by going to +Add in the menu and clicking on "DNA Test Information." WikiTree supports all of the major DNA testing companies, yourDNAportal, as well as allowing you to add information for any other testing company. You are also encouraged to enter your Y-DNA or mtDNA haplogroups.

Before upgrading from guest membership, you are asked to enter tags based on your genealogy interests. For those searching for family, surnames are an obvious choice for tags. Surname tags are a great way to bring those searching for family to the attention of other members at WikiTree. When a member enters a surname tag, other members following that tag will receive an email notification. They will often pop on over to say hello and to see what tree and DNA test information may already be added for the member.

Having all the DNA test information, surname tags, and any biographical information all front and center on a member's profile makes it easier for other members to help those who are searching.

We Collaborate

One of the major reasons the DNA features at WikiTree are so successful, is collaboration is one of the driving forces for the website. WikiTree is set up in such a way that encourages members to interact with and help one another all with the goal of growing an accurate one-world tree. And because all members who are related share the same ancestor profiles, instead of having

dozens of separate trees each member is working on, all descendants will work together to improve their shared profiles. For those searching for family, having a pool of people to contact regarding a possible ancestor is inspiring.

G2G

WikiTree's g2g forum is an amazing place for members to get help on all aspects of DNA and research. Whether a member has a question about adoption, how DNA works, how to search for family, or researching a family of interest, other WikiTreers are willing to assist.

After Family is Identified

After birth parents have been identified is when the DNA magic can really begin. The features at WikiTree are most amazing when a family tree is attached to a member's profile. With the new family information, you can start building a tree one generation at a time. As the tree grows, the DNA test information will populate through the family profiles of six generations of your tree. (For YDNA and mtDNA tests, WikiTree will populate the information up to the earliest known male and female ancestor.) When potential relatives see the ancestor's profile, they will see your DNA test information listed on that profile and can contact you to compare DNA and swap or share family information. For those with YDNA and mtDNA tests, you can collaborate with others related to you who have also tested.

Acknowledgements

I want to send a huge thank you to my research team at WikiTree's Adoption Angels who are all as passionate as I am about finding birth parents for everyone who is seeking. Thanks to you, countless hours of hard work have collectively gone into helping hundreds of people find answers.

And always, thank you to Charlotte Shockey and Ryan, top members of my support team.

About the Author

Emmaline MacBeath is a genetic genealogist who has helped hundreds of people to find their birth parents. She believes everyone should have easy access to their biological family trees because there is power in knowing where you come from. She spends her days connecting enslaved Americans to their families and descendants.

She also writes young adult and kids fiction under the pen name Emmaline Rose.

You can learn more about her work at www.missinglinkdna.com

Clues

_____

_____

_____

_____

_____

_____

_____

_____

_____

_____

_____

_____

_____

_____

_____

_____

_____

_____

_____

Additional Journal Pages